REBEL WITH A CAUSE

REBEL
WITH
A CAUSE

RAY AVERY WITH PAUL LITTLE

RANDOM HOUSE
NEW ZEALAND

A RANDOM HOUSE BOOK published by Random House New Zealand
18 Poland Road, Glenfield, Auckland, New Zealand

For more information about our titles go to www.randomhouse.co.nz

A catalogue record for this book is available from the National Library of
New Zealand

Random House New Zealand is part of the Random House Group
New York   London   Sydney   Auckland   Delhi   Johannesburg

First published 2010, reprinted 2010 (four times)

ISBN 978 1 86979 391 3

FSC
Mixed Sources
Product group from well-managed
forests and other controlled sources
Cert no. SCS-COC-001217
www.fsc.org
©1996 Forest Stewardship Council

Cover photograph: Jane Ussher
Cover design: Pieta Brenton
Text design: Saskia Nicol
Printed in New Zealand by Printlink

For Anna, Amelia and all the crazy ones.

FOREWORD

In early 2010 it was my great privilege to present scientist and extraordinary Kiwi Ray Avery with the inaugural Kiwibank New Zealander of the Year Award. Ray's efforts to fight poverty and ill health in the developing world made him a truly deserving winner. This award recognised his outstanding contribution to our nation and to the many millions of people in the developing world. Many people have Ray to thank for their improved opportunities in life, or the fact that they have survived illness or injury, from his relentless passion to address the social disparities of healthcare around the world.

In this book Ray reveals his journey from streetkid to global influencer. He is making a remarkable contribution to the human family, assisting up to 30 million blind people throughout the world. His willingness to challenge the status quo led him to establish his laboratories in Eritrea and Nepal which now provide

13 per cent of the world market for intraocular lenses. Their output has collapsed the cost of these precious items forever, making them affordable to the poorest of the poor.

When I met Ray I was impressed by his passion and drive. He is a remarkable person who embodies our Kiwi spirit. While he is the first to admit to being no saint, Ray sees problems as opportunities to make things better for those who aren't in a position to help themselves.

What struck me was his extraordinary commitment to leadership. It is even more inspiring when you consider the challenges he faced in his early years.

For Ray, family was a word that didn't demonstrate love, care and protection. Ray chose not to be the same. He had another vision. He wanted to change the world by supporting others, especially those who cannot protect themselves. This is a true testament to his inner strength and character.

Medicine Mondiale, the not-for-profit aid organisation he set up, is the manifestation of this commitment to change the world. In the unlikely location of Ray's Auckland garage is a high-tech lab that is addressing, in typical Kiwi can-do attitude, many of the health problems in the developing world.

This book is touching and humorous. The emotions it evokes make it an inspiring read. Ray's story shows that one man from New Zealand can truly change the world.

Rt Hon Jim Bolger
Patron New Zealander of the Year
Kiwibank Chair
August 2010

CONTENTS

PROLOGUE

In 1973 I travelled with some backpackers overland from the UK through Europe to Asia. One day, in Amritsar, in the Punjab, some of the girls came back to the bus in a state of high excitement. 'We have just found the most fantastic guru,' they said. 'You really need to go and see him.'

The guru was obviously a man of wisdom, because he had stationed himself on the roof of a temple where he could clearly be seen from a nearby café which was the local hotspot for itinerant backpackers. This was the sort of chai shop that sold fried banana fritters to cater for the sixties flower-power children.

Not expecting much, I decided to find out what he had to say, and ended up late one evening sitting cross-legged opposite him on a hot roof.

'You are on a long journey,' he said.

Well, yes. He could see the bus parked in the courtyard below. But then he told me this story from the *Bhagavad-Gita*.

There was once a woman who had a son who she loved very much and wanted to be happy. So she went to a guru who agreed to grant her one wish for her son.

'Choose carefully,' said the guru, 'for you will only have one wish and you will have to live with its consequences.'

The woman thought for a long time before finding what she thought was the perfect wish.

'I wish that everyone he meets will always love my son,' she said.

'Are you sure that is what you wish?' asked the guru.

'Yes, yes.'

'So be it.'

And the woman went hurrying to find her son, but when she got to him she saw him surrounded by a throng of people, stroking him, kissing him, crowding around him and preventing him from moving. He looked as miserable as it is possible for a person to look.

The woman rushed back to the guru.

'I have made a terrible mistake,' she said. 'I need you to grant me another wish.'

'I am sorry,' said the guru, 'but I told you I could only give you one wish. There is nothing I can do.'

The woman wailed and begged and pleaded and finally the guru relented.

'Very well. Think of another wish for your son and if it is the right one, I will grant it. If it is not, then things

will stay as they are.'

The anxious mother thought for a long time.

'I wish,' she said finally, 'for my son to love everyone he meets.'

'That is the correct wish,' said the guru. 'It is granted.'

When the mother found her son again, he was walking through a crowd of people. Most were ignoring him, others shoved him as they passed by, one even took offence at something and spat on him. But his eyes were full of love and his face had a look of total contentment.

The rooftop guru of Amritsar may have been speculative in the stories he told to the transient flower-power children who hung on his every word, but for me he spoke the absolute truth, although it would be some time before I totally understood it.

I spent the first part of my life trying to make people love me, and often failing, starting with my parents. Much later in life, thanks to a chance encounter with the brilliant Fred Hollows and some remarkable people in the developing world, I learnt how to truly love others, and every blessing I ever wished for came to me. Now I spend my time putting that love to practical use, changing the world, and this book is the story of how that became my goal.

ONE

Never a close family

I got married for the first and only time when I was sixty, and had my first child when I was sixty-one. If I spent more years than most people looking for love and a family, it was because my own parents hadn't provided the sort of loving environment that will grow a healthy human being.

My father's name was Cyril William Raymond John Avery and my mother's was Annie Bailey and as a pair they were toxic. They should have split up the moment they got together. They didn't want me, and I don't have a single good memory of either of them.

I was born in 1947, the product of a post-war fling. My father had been in the ill-fated 1940 British Expeditionary Force and was captured at the Franco-Belgian border. He was held in Polish prison camps, being marched from one to another for most of World War II. He was obviously a survivor but I think the war affected him in ways we never realised.

He was a charismatic character with a killer smile that I've inherited. And I think he probably felt that he deserved a day out after five years of hell. There's no doubt he enjoyed life and lived large.

When he and my mother met, they didn't start living together for a while. When I came along, they wanted to be together but not with a baby around. Before I left the cot I was being farmed out to a succession of relatives so they could get on with the partying. I don't remember much . . . a constantly changing sea of faces and long twilight walks up crunchy gravel paths, pulling the blankets up to my chin in a strange new bed in strange new surroundings.

The only toys I ever had came from kindly folk who we called aunties and uncles, even though they were not blood relations. My mum and dad weren't big on toys and teddy bears. I don't remember ever having any toys of my own to play with, but occasionally there were some at the houses where I stayed, and I was told to take one or was given it when I was leaving for one of the occasional spells back living with my mother.

But those teddy bears always seemed to smell funny and I'd discard them somewhere along the way home. That home was a classic terraced house on the Canterbury City Council housing estate.

On my birth certificate my father is described as an agricultural worker but he really earned his living as a handyman — doing jobs at people's houses, building walls, painting. He also had a big flash car he used as a taxi.

'I've got a really good fare,' he often told my mother. 'Someone's going to pay me to drive them all the way to Cornwall.' But the really good fare always required him to be away for the weekend or overnight. And no one ever saw any money at the end of it, so when he came back there was a fight and on it went. My mother was addicted to tobacco, alcohol and violence.

My father was a career womaniser. I saw him every day parked at the local taxi rank when I was walking to school. There was always a different woman sitting in the car with him. There was a supermarket on the corner near the rank and he wandered around there and picked up women. And although it wasn't as bad as my mother's on a day-to-day basis, he also had a violent streak.

Once, I was riding my bike down the hill outside our house. I had a flag attached to the front wheel and I wanted to see how fast I could make the flag flutter. I was so intent on this I forgot to brake at the intersection at the end of the road and slammed into a wall, buckling the front wheel. I picked myself up and eventually managed to wheel the wobbling bike all the way back home. When my father saw it he exploded in a paroxysm of anger.

'You're fucking hopeless,' he yelled and started jumping up and down on the wheels of the bike, making spaghetti out of the spokes. In a few moments he destroyed the whole thing and threw the bits across our combination junkyard and back garden. He killed my bike.

He was unpredictable. At other times he drove me to school, showing me off like a trophy. If there was a woman he had his eye on and wanted to impress, he made sure she saw him being the good father. The next day he disappeared and was not seen again for weeks or months.

I know the police were aware of my parents, because I once

happened to see a record sheet which listed a huge number of call-outs involving them.

Like the time my mother locked herself in the bathroom and my father tried to break down the door with a claw hammer. When this didn't work he got an axe and started hacking at the lock. She jumped out the window, broke a leg and had to go to hospital. My father took off because the cops were looking for him, leaving me to look after my mum and her leg.

On another occasion in the dead of the English winter my father woke me up in the middle of the night because he was doing some moonlighting job and needed his trowel, which I had been playing with in the garden.

He dragged me barefoot into the snow in just my pyjama bottoms and started smacking me around the head.

'Where's the fucking trowel?' he yelled.

Eventually we found it and I was allowed to go back to bed. There was nothing surprising about this sort of behaviour by then, but when my dad lost it he went really out of control, and I was always worried that one day he would go too far and my mother or I would end up seriously hurt, if not dead.

I LOVED MY MUM because she was my mother, but there was no mother–son relationship. She never put the time in to make that happen. She was a stranger in a lot of ways, certainly for the first few years. Even after my parents split up I was farmed out as much as possible, but I always ended up being given back for one reason or another.

My mother was claiming a government benefit for me and when she got word the inspectors were coming around to check on the situation at home I was repatriated quick smart so she could still get her money.

Clothes were packed back in a brown leather suitcase with Avery scratched on the side when my mother needed me at home again. A handwritten address was tied by string to the handle and when it was finally clicked closed I thrust my little hand into the air to be led, stumbling away, behind big footsteps.

The only consistent thing in the relationship was the house itself. In my mind, I was going back to the house, not to my mum.

Every time I went back things were different. There might be a strange bloke living there; might be my father. You just got with the programme.

Cash was always a problem, which is why at one point my mother considered selling me. I had been fostered out to a couple who seemed really to love me. Their own son had been killed and they wanted a replacement, so they came around and spoke to my mother about a financial arrangement. Some negotiations went on, but in the end it fell through.

My father was supposed to be providing financial support when they had split up but never did. It was my job every Friday to go to the office that took care of these matters and collect the money he was supposed to have deposited. There was a counter and a woman behind it and she gave me an envelope and I took it home.

But if there was no money there and I went home empty-handed, my mother blamed me for it and I got a beating. I think she saw my father in me and hated me on his behalf. At least my mother's violence was predictable — in any situation there was a fifty-fifty chance of getting whacked, whereas my father's violent outbursts were more random and pathological.

Any good memories from those years are of things that took place outside the home and away from my parents. Usually they involved my early scientific experimenting and property damage with the local kids.

We were heavily influenced by the John Wayne-type war movies which played at the Saturday-morning pictures and on the TV in post-war Britain. With that as our background, and a little bit of science reading, we worked out how to make bombs.

There were lots of bomb sites around — empty spaces that had once been houses full of families, blasted into nothing by the Luftwaffe and now used as carparks. Underneath, however, there were still the old basements with holes opening into tunnels. We used these to hide away from the imperfect world above, and create our own imaginary world in the damp and dark passageways, which were the stage for our mock battles.

I decided to build an arsenal of explosives. Around Guy Fawkes time it was easy to get gunpowder. I took old bicycle handle bars, blocked one end and manufactured a mega mortar which propelled ball bearings nearly a hundred metres.

I could have killed someone but the worst I did was wreck a man's car when I was about seven. We were firing our homemade mortar at the Fibrolite shed roofs in the nearby allotment. There was a huge bang and the 'bullets' disappeared in the distance. Suddenly this man came running up to us, screaming his head off. We got taken down to his Fibro garage which was now pockmarked with Avery mortar shells and shown the car inside which looked like Swiss cheese.

We were lucky not to kill ourselves because these basements usually had only a small hole as their point of entry. If we set off a bomb or started a fire to keep warm, the room instantly filled with smoke and we scrambled to get out.

Explosions were a constant theme in our otherwise boring lives. Outside every house was a small inspection trap for turning off the gas to the property. There were rows and rows of terraced houses with one of these every few metres. We had a game where one kid walked along with a knife or screwdriver and flicked open the lid, and the one behind him threw in a match. Just enough gas built up over time to make a worthwhile and unpredictable bang. Once we were doing this with a third, much smaller, kid bringing up the rear. That was his job — to bring up the rear. At one house I threw the match in but there was a gas leak and as this kid got level there was a great boom and he was shot into the air. We gathered him up and ran back to his house with him, rang the doorbell and ran away, leaving the smouldering and dazed cargo to be discovered by his loving mother.

Not surprisingly, after a time, other kids in the street weren't allowed to play with me because I was so creatively dangerous. I was fascinated by all kinds of weapons. Having read lots of Robin Hood books I decided to create Sherwood Forest in our council housing estate. Metal dustbin lids with handles made perfect shields, and all we needed were a few fence palings from the bowling green down the road to make passable swords. In the local woods was a willow tree with suckers that we used to make perfect arrows, using traditional techniques from Norman days. Before you knew it we had a full-blown 1066 battle scene being played out from one end of the street to the other. There were a lot of bruised knuckles and bruised heads but no one lost an eye.

Nobody taught me these things. I was teaching myself about applied science. I could work out how to do all sorts of things on the street, but at home I still couldn't work out how to make my mother love me. As I got older, I tried to win her love by doing things for her. Every night, she had to walk three or four kilometres home from the hospital where she worked as a cleaner and I walked to meet her after school, often getting halfway there before she did. Sometimes she might be pleased to see me, sometimes she was angry with me. There was no way of predicting. Whatever I did, it didn't really make any difference, but I kept trying.

At home it was my job to get the fire going and get the Epsom salts out in a basin so she could soak her feet after work. I thought if I made her feel loved she wouldn't keep kicking the living crap out of me.

I was always alone, even when I was at home. I didn't have any long meaningful conversations with her. She just barked out orders. If she wanted a pack of cigarettes at 10pm at night she woke me up and I had to get dressed and go down to the pub to buy them.

I didn't even like to sit downstairs with her in the evenings because it always ended badly. Something unpredictable set her off and she exploded. Or someone came around and it was better to be upstairs in my own space.

I expanded my bedroom and library into the attic space above to get away from people. I had a special lock on my door and I rejigged a bolt on the inside, using a fishing wire and a hook and nail that I could flick into position from the outside. My mum didn't know what I had done. She couldn't get into my room, but she didn't know why. I could lock myself in and then get into the attic or out the window, down the drainpipe and go off somewhere.

If she had a gentleman friend around there was no supper, so it wasn't worth coming downstairs anyway. I went off for walks around the streets to see what the world was like.

Or I lost myself writing in my notebook. My books were like an artwork. I got *World Digest* comics and taught myself how to draw, in pencil particularly, because you could use the graphite to produce wonderfully subtle shading effects. I tried to get the shading right when copying a horse and became completely absorbed. It took me away from everything. Books stimulated my imagination but drawing consumed even more of my senses. I probably had ten goes at the same thing. I did one and then the next one and then looked at it to see if I was improving. That absorption was absolute joy.

I didn't know at the time how lucky I was to have the luxury of my own room with my little collection of electronics gear and other treasures. I stayed in there hoping the adults would forget about me, which they usually did.

Those are the best childhood memories I have. There are no special moments with either of my parents to look back on fondly. My father certainly wasn't around long enough to pass on any skills to me.

Fortunately, all that time spent alone got me started out on a path of experimenting and self-sufficiency that has allowed me to do what I do today. I suppose we could have gone on like this until eventually I was legally old enough to leave home and take care of myself. But it didn't take that long. It all came to a head over the eggs.

AT THE HOSPITAL where my mother worked, fish was delivered daily on large flat wooden trays. She brought the trays home because they were free and made good kindling. They were free because they stank of fish. We had piles of them in the back garden and the neighbours used to complain about the smell all the time.

One of my jobs was to chop them up for kindling. As well as the fishy wood, our fuel was some dodgy coal that my father had delivered from someone he knew. Our back garden consisted of kindling, coal and car parts from various vehicles that he was pulling apart, and of course the remains of my broken bike.

There was a mealtime routine for when I was at school and my mother was working. Dinner was supposed to be at 5pm but she didn't get home until 6pm. So she cooked the meal before she went to work and it was always the same: last night's leftovers plus fried bread and fried egg.

Fortunately, I had a paper round which gave me some disposable income and my first sense of freedom. I could afford to buy the odd burger or a roll or sweets.

But more often than not, I'd just go into the local cake shop. I worked out this routine.

'Have you got any stale buns?' I asked them on the first day I tried this.

'No, off you go,' one snapped. I had a school uniform on, so I obviously wasn't destitute.

I outwaited them. I put on a down-in-the-mouth face and went and sat on a seat outside the shop. I waited until they had turned the lights off and gone home, but I knew they had seen me still sitting there as they were leaving.

That went on for about two days before they capitulated and I got some stale rolls. Then it became a regular thing to wait for the stale rolls. After a while, they started giving me food the moment I appeared. I graduated to biscuits.

Sometimes I paid or tried to pay and then they gave me my money back. I had my roll and I collected a stash of biscuits and baking that I kept in the attic so if I was upstairs reading books away from my mother and all the palaver going on downstairs I didn't go hungry.

But I could not eat the fried egg and bread my mother made

and left for me. After it had been sitting in the house all day getting cold it ended up looking like it had congealed pus all over the top of it, and heating it up just made it worse. It was awful. I'd take it straight outside, climb over the fish boxes and scrape it all under the hedge at the back of the section beside the next house.

During one period when my father had taken off again and I was responsible for the manly things of the house, I was outside chopping up the kindling to light the fire when my mother came home.

She came out the back with the coal scuttle for me to fill up and she started wandering absent-mindedly around the garden. She went up to the hedge where there were a whole lot of weeds hanging out. She started to pull them out and when she did she saw about a year's worth of fried eggs. The freaky thing about them was that they hadn't rotted; they were covered in oil and they just sat there like they were permanently embalmed.

She cracked.

She picked up one of the pine boards from the crate I was working on and started smacking me around the head. She was ferocious. It was worse than anything she had ever done to me before. It was even worse than anything my dad had ever done to me.

'You bastard,' she yelled, hitting me to punctuate her rant. 'You little shit! I clean and cook every day for you, put food on the table and you just throw it away.' I curled up in a foetal position and put my hands over my head to protect myself while she smacked the stuffing out of me. Eventually she knocked me unconscious.

I suppose she could have just dragged me inside and left me there, hoping I would get better, but thankfully she didn't. She took me to the hospital. At the A&E they took one look at me and called the cops, who of course knew about our family already because of my parents' fights.

In those cases she had always blamed my father for the violence, but she couldn't do that this time.

The cops interviewed her first. When I regained consciousness in the men's ward with a bandage around my head, a fracture behind my ear and three broken fingers, one of those nice robust women with surgical stockings and a notepad came and sat next to me and asked me what had happened.

One might have imagined that, in a case like this, when it's your mum and you love her, you never portray her in a bad light. Blood is thicker than water and all that.

'She hits me all the time,' I said.

The woman didn't pause for a moment.

'We're going to take you into protective care,' she explained, 'and you won't see your mother until the court has decided what's going to happen to you.'

And I was made a ward of the court and never spent another night under the same roof as my mother. I was nine years old. In reality, though, during those nine years, I had spent only a couple in total living with her.

So far as I know, she never tried to make contact with me after I was made a ward of the court. I know many people think: 'Well, you lived with her, and she was your mum, why didn't you try and track her down?'

There are two reasons. One is the reason for which I was made a ward of the court — she had beaten me senseless. And from a legal perspective, the deal was that there was to be no contact. Steps were taken to keep me protected from her.

Of course, I knew where the house was and went back there

about eighteen months later, but she had moved in with some bloke who lived in a nearby village.

Mum was a bit like my father in that respect — even though she had her job at the hospital, if a bloke came along and took her fancy, she disappeared with him for stretches of time and I was left alone for a week or so.

I'd always looked after myself, even that young. I don't consider I had a family.

My father, however, I did see again. He arranged a strange meeting when I was a teenager. He suddenly appeared at Wye College, where I was working. The woman he was living with was a nurse and had heard that I existed. She was a nice woman and wanted to meet me.

So at her instigation the three of us had this very strange meeting in a coffee bar in Wye. I was doing quite well by then and looked the part, and my father was as proud as punch because I was this smart little bloke.

'Well, we'll keep in touch,' he said at the end, 'now we know where you are.'

And that was it. It was bizarre. That was the last time I ever saw him.

BOTH MY PARENTS are dead now. I don't know exactly when my mother died, only that she did. I found out because I went back to England twenty years later for the Fred Hollows Foundation and got a story in the *Kent Herald* to get publicity for the foundation. A half-sister, my father's daughter, saw it, tracked me down and wrote to me.

She wanted me to meet my father and said in passing, 'As you know, your mother died.' And that was how I found out. She had got together with another man and had a baby and there were complications, as a result of which she died.

The only time I ever had a family feeling about any blood relatives was when I wondered what happened to that kid. I thought maybe I could make sure they didn't have a fractured childhood like mine. But I knew that wouldn't work. By then I had survived years of fostering, when people had rented me in the belief they were going to get a replacement son, and I was probably just hoping to get a new brother or sister. It couldn't have worked out anyway, because I was still trying to find out who I was.

I thought it was telling that a woman I didn't know was saying, 'Your dad wants to make contact with you,' rather than a letter or call from my father.

I replied and said, 'I've moved on. Unfortunately I'm now back in New Zealand and I travel a lot internationally, so I don't think there's any chance of catching up in the foreseeable future.'

Then I got a letter sent to the Fred Hollows Foundation from my dad, saying, 'I'm quite sick. I've had my hip replaced and I'm not expected to last for another six months, and it'd be nice for you to come and meet.'

At that time I wasn't about to dig deep and find some forgiveness for him, after what I had been through, just to make him feel better.

A lot of people I have told that to have been a bit shocked and said, 'Oh, but he was your father.' But, then and now, I can't peel back, condone or erase fourteen years of absolute terror and abuse.

My father was in his eighties when he died, and he still didn't get it. He even said in his last letter, apparently without seeing any irony: 'I know we were never a close family.'

TWO

No *place like home*

The next few years saw me shuttled back and forth between foster homes and orphanages, with spells at halfway houses in between. In post-war England this wasn't unusual. I was one of tens of thousands who made up a forgotten generation as a result of the war.

Some of that generation were genuine orphans, being sent around the country in the hope they could find a new life, and some were sent to Australia and New Zealand to be fostered out. In the last eighteen months of the war, when the bombing was at its worst, about 300,000 kids were moved from their own homes to safe locations in the provinces that weren't being targeted. They were packed on buses and sent away to big houses that were requisitioned for the job.

Some parents who stayed behind in London were killed,

and it was assumed those kids had no relatives. There was an acceptance when you were in that structure that you didn't have any family of your own, whether your parents were alive or dead. That's why it was so easy to disappear into the system.

Other kids, like me, were the product of post-war romances that should never have happened, when soldiers came back after years away and a huge number of babies were born. By the time we were six or seven, nobody really wanted to have us full-time, so we were farmed out to whoever would take us.

The first thing I had to get used to was the institutionalisation. Previously, I had a lot of freedom that I had made for myself because my mother didn't really care what I got up to. But I was also well trained in behaving so as not to get into trouble.

Establishments like orphanages are only able to function by dehumanising people so they will work as a single unit. That meant, for instance, waking, dressing and eating at the same time and being dressed the same as everyone else. Some of the places were funded by returned servicemen's associations. The uniform was military grey in a heavy, coarse material. Grey jackets. Grey socks. Grey skin in many cases. And one pair of brown shoes. When that pair got buggered, you were allowed another pair. Three pairs of socks. Three pairs of underpants. Two pairs of shorts. And three shirts. It was impossible to display any individuality.

You wore your shirts for five days and washed them once a week. After you got dressed there was an inspection with one of the male staff adjusting your long socks or anything else out of place. And you hoped that was all he was going to do.

You spent the rest of the day as part of a process. There was a prayer at the start of the day — a touch of religion, which was supposed to be the justification behind the whole exercise. Then we went down to breakfast of porridge, toast, jam and semolina. Next we went to assembly and sang a few songs — 'All Things Bright and Beautiful' was almost inevitable — and then we were piled into buses to be taken to our different schools.

They liked to keep you at the same school as much as possible. At least it meant some continuity when you got kicked out of a foster home or ran away from the orphanage and got sent to live somewhere else. Your new accommodation had to be more than eighty kilometres from your old school before they would consider sending you to a new school.

Bus tickets and train tickets were supplied and that was great for me. Trains became a way of life very early on and would play an important part in my childhood years. When I wanted to run away it wasn't very complicated, because I was used to just jumping on a train.

One of the things I loved about them was that the carriages were divided into compartments and you could walk along the platform until you found an empty one and have your own space. Sometimes I got on trains and just rode wherever they were going, or up and down a line all day.

It wasn't hard to talk your way onto a platform.

'I'm just looking for my mum,' I said if anyone asked what I was doing.

It was glorious in summer when you could put the window down and feel the breeze. Even better if you had money in your pocket. Usually I took food with me but once I forgot and all I had was twenty pence. I managed to find some sweets I could buy for that much and they were the most delicious sweets I ever tasted. I learnt my lesson about planning. If I was going to run away I would need serious preparation.

I knew one place where there was a huge orchard about 100

metres from the train station. Because they employed fruit pickers, there were also toilet blocks and other facilities, which was good because I filled my belly with so much fruit I ended up spending a lot of time on the toilet. I could hide for two or three days there quite comfortably if the weather was warm and relish the purity of my own existence.

SOMETHING I ESPECIALLY hated about the institutions was how, at night, whether you were seven or twelve years old, at eight or nine o'clock, when it was lights-out time, the lights went out. They would dim slowly and then blackness, no matter what you might be doing.

In some places, they also locked the door, which was dangerous and probably illegal. It solved the problem of kids getting out and roaming around, but it also meant you couldn't even go to the toilet unless you were game enough to squat down between the rows of beds and use one of the potties, which would open a Pandora's box of problems. You could ring the bell, but that would probably bring you more trouble than your original problem was worth.

I would have loved to sneak out for a walk, particularly in summer, but you would always get found out and be caned for it. I learnt not to buck the system. The best thing you could do was play by the rules and try to be anonymous.

Some of the homes were run mainly by women, but a lot were staffed by men who were doing it only because they had come back from the war needing a job. I remember a lot of tattooed guys. It seemed they went overseas, shot some people, got a few tattoos and came back again.

And in those days the majority of them had a fag hanging out of their mouths most of the time. Anyone who knows anything about abuse will tell you that one of the things you remember most is smells, and I remember the smell of these cigarettes very vividly.

Since those times there have been a lot of exposés about what goes on in these institutions, and they were nirvana for paedophiles. I found a lot of it hard to understand. I didn't know the difference between somebody genuinely adjusting my long socks and someone who lingered too long around a particular area. To some degree we were all looking for love, and if somebody showed it to me then I probably thought that was a good thing until something bad happened. My innate distrust of pretty much everybody merely got deeper.

Once, in Canterbury, years later, when I was the man about town with my flash sports car, handmade shoes and sharp clothes, I was walking down the street and saw a bloke who had abused me in one of the hostels and my reaction amazed me. I was big enough, tough enough and old enough and should have been confident enough to confront him. But those people have a power over you that never goes away, because of all the underlying things that made it possible in the first place. What went on all those years before comes straight back, and all you can do is put it in a box and put a lid on it and keep going. I kept going.

Those experiences are why I sought the company of women so avidly — because even with all that my mother had done, I found them safe compared to men. They were soft and gentle and sometimes there would be some of the love and warmth that I desperately wanted.

I had a romantic image of women — one woman in particular — in my head from very early on. When I was reading under the covers with my torch, I would devour anything from Chaucer to women's magazines and they would often have romantic passages about love and falling in love.

I imagined what the woman I would fall in love with was going to be like. She was going to wear a white dress, she would make my heart melt when she first appeared and I was going to be helping her across a stream and there would probably be a few Bambis strolling around in the background. That was the perfect picture in my head. It would take fifty years to find, but it did come true.

Sometimes, whether because I had run away from a foster home once too often or simply because there was nowhere else to send me, I would end up in places that were little more than borstals, thrown in with kids who were there for stabbing people and worse.

In those dormitories, life was a multi-dimensional reign of terror — you were at risk of abuse from caregivers outside and gangs of boys inside. The longer the others had been there, the stronger their gang was and the more trouble you were up for when you arrived. I discovered quickly that the more people there are trying to kick the living daylights out of you the better off you are because there's no room for them to work up a good swing. If it is just two or three you're going to end up with some serious damage.

I learnt to stand up for myself early on. Every time I went into a new dormitory the resident bully would be straight off the rank to make sure I knew who was boss. So I had to show him — and anyone else who might be thinking of having a go — that I was more dangerous than anybody else they had ever seen in their lives. And I had to do it as soon as possible.

Once I arrived in a dormitory at night and got put into bed straight away. Being in bed in a dormitory is really scary anyway, because if it's cold and you've got your paws under the blankets, there's no way you can get them out fast enough if someone smacks you. In a new place, it's even scarier. This time, I had only been in bed a little while when suddenly there was a crack to the skull and a guy was on top of me with his knees on my shoulders, punching my head and beating the crap out of me.

'Do you give in? Do you give in?'

'Yes. Yes.'

Of course I gave in.

This place had a cottage garden where we grew vegetables. Not long after this attack I was down there when this guy came around a corner of the gardening shed and smacked his chest straight into the flat of my shovel. He dropped to the floor and I broke both of his legs with the handle of the shovel. No one bothered me again.

Back in bed I slept fitfully because every noise sounded like a threat.

Added to all this was the uncertainty of not knowing how long I was going to be in a particular place or where I was going to be sent next.

I made myself a flick knife for protection. It was a big, intimidating thing that you could open and fix in position. Unfortunately, it didn't have a spring to make it a proper flick knife, so, in the metalwork shop when no one was looking, I carved the necessary bits off to let it be floppy. I could hold it closed then flick it so the blade came out and locked. I practised and practised with it.

It's not quite as dramatic as it sounds. Lots of kids played a game called splits. Two of you stood opposite each other with your legs apart. You threw a knife to their right and they had to stretch their leg out to where it landed. Then one to the left, and so on, getting further each time. We were used to knives.

In every situation I've encountered, I've developed what in science and business we call Standard Operating Procedures or SOPs — it's the simplest, most effective way of doing anything, broken down into simple individual steps. My first SOP was probably my efforts to keep my mother happy.

When it came to bullies, my SOP was to create the impression that I was harder than they were right from the start. It was harder for me to do this because the thing I liked most was to sit on my bed reading. When I got to a new place I tried to get to the dormitory before all the others and set myself up so that when they arrived I was already reading my book and could ignore them.

But there was always one who didn't want to be ignored, and once he made his move I produced my knife and stabbed whatever was closest. It might have been the bed or it might have been the book. But it was saying, 'I'm crazy. Stay away.' It helped that I was so scared that my terrified shaking came across like psychotic trembling.

Eventually, I realised that the real psychopaths didn't care if you had a knife or not. They would smack you anyway. The knife was only useful for scaring away the amateurs. But I don't think I would ever have stabbed anyone unless my life actually depended on it. It was just part of the SOP.

Boys would find opportunities to bully each other in any situation. One favourite technique was to walk up behind you and stand on the back of your shoe to make it come off. Then it was all on. I learnt the smartest thing to do was turn around and hit the biggest guy there several times as fast as I could, again and again until it was past brutal. The idea, again, was to make everyone think you were a psychopath so they would leave you alone. The alternative was a road to perdition and degradation.

Another big part of my SOP was running away if things got too bad. At one orphanage I got a hell of a beating after I had been there less than 24 hours. I could see there was no way I was going to be able to stop it happening again.

The dormitory was on the second storey, and it was one of those where you got locked in, but I was determined, and I managed to prise away the hook on the window that was there to stop it opening too far. I jumped out and landed okay, except that when I hit the ground my knees connected with my chin and I nearly bit through my tongue.

With blood pouring from my mouth I got carted off to hospital, but I also got out of that place.

DURING THIS TIME I mostly kept going to school just like other kids. I actually liked lessons. Back in primary school there was one report that summed things up and I think always remained true: 'Ray Avery has got the right attitude to work and will do well.' Another observation I remember and can see the truth of was: 'Ray Avery is very good at mental arithmetic as long as he can write it down.' I had to work extra hard in class because my sight and hearing weren't good and being dyslexic was just a bonus. I was always asking teachers for extra notes and help, and I think that got me some credit.

But there were other problems with school. I got caned so many times for so many reasons, many of them things no one would even notice today.

I naturally played the fool because laughter was the greatest weapon I had against the caustic nature of my existence and I would express it without thinking. I liked English literature a lot, but if we were looking at Dickens, for example, and I was asked to read aloud I would improvise to make the other kids laugh, and that laughter would end with me getting the cane.

One year, we had a geography teacher whose first name was Stella. This was 1950s England and teachers were terribly Dickensian, sterile and serious people. We had a cricket match between staff and students one year and Stella hit a six, much to everyone's surprise. I yelled out: 'Go, Stella.' And I got the cane for that.

I loved acquiring knowledge but I hated the discipline of school, especially once the habit of resisting any kind of regimentation had been established.

At my secondary school, Frank Hooker — they changed the name later — we were divided into 'houses' with names like Becket and Cranmer, and with 'house masters', and every morning there was a house meeting, which seemed to me like a pointless attempt to indoctrinate working-class kids with upper-class values.

The pressure not to be an individual was so great that I took every opportunity I could find to demonstrate my independence. Once, in religious instruction class, the teacher asked us: 'Why did Moses lead the Israelites into the Promised Land?' And I said, 'Because they didn't have porridge sandwiches,' and I got caned for it.

At secondary school, chemistry was a class I took seriously, and I was positively fascist about keeping great notes. I wrote down all the experiments in nice rounded handwriting in a big thick notebook. There would only have been about six words to the line because I was doing a lot of drawing and painting at the time and loved the way words looked.

Our work was done using pens filled from an ink well. One day, the guy next to me deliberately nudged me so that my pen went right across my beautiful page. I took the pen and squirted it all over his pages, and there was a huge scuffle, and we got the cane for that.

I loved technical drawing because it was a bit of art and a bit of science, the two things I loved most. And I loved doing experiments. One we had used a vertical ball race to measure the amount of energy released in a small explosion made using nitrogen trioxide paper. You put the paper under a base and dropped the ball on it and measured how far it went up a fixed track.

The bangs we were getting weren't enough for me, so when the teacher was out of the room I got ten pieces of the paper and put them under the base.

When he came back, he did the experiment, dropping the ball on the paper. Because there was so much paper it didn't really bounce, so he dropped it again from a much greater height and the whole thing blew up and shot to the ceiling. They made us sit there till I owned up and I got the cane for that.

I had worked out it was better to own up. You always got caned anyway, but if you got the others into trouble they got stuck into you as well, so you copped it twice.

I didn't make close friends at school. It seemed to be a floating population, so even when I was going regularly, other people seemed to come and go all the time. I skulked off every chance I got to somewhere I could sit and read my book and learn stuff. I preferred that to joining in what I considered to be a lot of screaming and shouting or getting into fractious situations. In the meantime I was also looking after my own education away from school. By the time I was about six or seven, I was taking myself off to science museums or the Tate Gallery to learn more about my two passions.

I had to look after myself because there was no one to look out for me. I didn't even have a voice. I realised that for the first time one day at primary school, and it was very hard to deal with. When you don't have a voice, no one is going to listen to you.

It was a race day at primary school. As all of those primary-school sports days are, it was totally disorganised. I was in the 100-yard dash, which I was pretty good at. There weren't enough teachers to monitor who came in first and second and so on, so it was left up to the parents. We ran the race and I came in third, at least, out of eighteen kids. But when the parents saw the kids coming in they couldn't remember where any other kids were — just their own. By the time they had all got their own kids' names on the form, there was only eighteenth place left and that was me. I was really shocked and pissed off. I had tried hard to win and nobody cared. That was the first time I was really aware that if you don't have a voice then you can't rely on the morality of the general population to come to your rescue.

Not having a mum or dad was also the reason I didn't do some basic early exams. There was nobody to make sure I went through the system.

VIOLENCE AND UNFAIRNESS weren't confined to dormitories and classrooms. The foster homes were also full of both. Those experiences are part of the reason I work to help people in the developing world and give them a fair go — because they have been left behind too, and they don't have a voice. They are orphans with no one to look after them. But I can, and I will, otherwise my hard-won moral education and freedom will have been wasted.

I was constantly confronted with the potential for huge violence in all of us. That's why I hate it so much and stay calm these days when bad things happen. I have seen too many people lose their self-control. They will justify any kind of outburst, but when they get to that point, something is seriously wrong. If you took ownership of all that as a child, and accepted responsibility for adults' crazy behaviour, then you would be really screwed up.

There was one family where the father challenged moral logic, although most of the time it was one of the nicer places. There were three other boys, the house was big and the mother cooked good food. But the father went down to the pub every night and got legless and then came back and started shouting and banging around the place.

He always wanted a drink of milk before he went to bed and sometimes there wasn't any. I'm not sure who drank the milk; it could have been one of us or all of us. It might have been that I was meant to get the milk but the paper round took too long and by the time I got to the shop it was too late. For whatever reason, when it wasn't there he went off. He called us a pack of bastards and came into our bedroom and flung the empty bottle at the nearest kid. You got brained, it smashed and there would be all the cleaning up to do.

He did this one Christmas Eve, and then on Christmas morning we woke up and he had got us each a new pair of shoes. I found that kind of contradiction between being a good bloke and being violent impossible to deal with.

But there wasn't a lot I could do to stop anyone being violent or the victim of violence. And although I knew what to expect at school and in the institutions, there was never any predicting what I would find when I went to one of the countless foster homes I was sent to after I was made a ward of court.

There was always a possibility that one of them would become a permanent home, but it never happened. One reason was that

I had already learnt not to trust anyone's emotions. I was ready for them to turn on me at any time. That meant I didn't give a lot of myself either, so couldn't have a proper relationship, even with the good people I stayed with.

As I got older it became more difficult to place me, because people didn't want older kids. That meant having to go into halfway accommodation which was a maximum of three months. At the end of that time I was turned in. I was always aware that it wasn't going to last and I always felt like an outsider. So many people who were supposed to look after me had let me down that I had no faith in humanity.

For instance, behaviour that might have been perfectly natural and loving, such as somebody opening the door when you've gone to bed to check you are okay, I would interpret as meaning something bad was going to happen. That must have adversely pervaded my demeanour in terms of the way I related to them.

The whole premise of dropping a strange child into an existing family was unnatural. Perhaps with a modern family that was well off and had well-adjusted kids it might work. But not in poor families in post-war Britain, where there was an excess of children and not enough places for them to stay.

My SOP for foster homes was the usual: I thought if I was good and helped with the housework, then they would treat me well. I was armed with a good kit when I went into those places, because at home with my mother I had to get that family fire going before she got back from work. I was very useful. I was an expert at chopping wood and using newspaper to put up against the fire and get it drawing. I tried to help and be a good diligent person, but often that didn't even register because the agenda in the household was something quite different.

Sometimes you were just fresh meat, a target for abuse. Other people were fostering as a revenue stream. They would take kids and put them in spaces little bigger than a large cupboard or in rooms where as many as six of us were crammed in an area big enough for two.

An example of the revenue stream attitude was a woman who had been quite well off but fallen on hard times. Her husband was a banker who was killed in the war. She had a son, about fifteen, who was her pride and joy. One night, she left me with a drink and some bread and jam while they went out. After I had finished I took myself out for a walk and found them sitting in a café having a lovely tea. That happened more than once and I ran away from that home too, not because I was being abused but because it was just so wrong I couldn't be a party to it. She was getting good money to feed me and she wasn't.

As an income source, I was just as much part of a process as I was in an orphanage. Up in the morning for a dollop of porridge, then off to school and home for spam at night. There was no playing Monopoly beside the fire.

When I arrived somewhere new, I was treated with suspicion because those already there saw me as competition for food and resources. You couldn't make friends with the other boys even if you wanted to. One of the results of the policy of keeping us at our old schools was that you didn't go to school with the kids you were living with. And they came and went from the homes seemingly at random. One day they were living there, the next day they weren't.

The group decided where I was going to fit in the hierarchy. I had no real control of my life at all. It seemed all right for a couple of nights, but then one of these guys decided to climb into your bed and that stuffed it all up. And he was bigger than you, so to get out you had to run away.

Running away was my speciality. I did it because it got me out of one place and into the next. But it also worked against me because I got a reputation as a problem kid, which meant I was put with the toughest families rather than the ones I might have been a success with.

I took a change of clothes and whatever books and pencils I had. The trick was to make sure that they didn't know I was running away, so there was no stockpiling of stuff. The most important thing was to have the writing material, because that would occupy me.

If it was summer I might find a nice cornfield and lie there sketching in the sun, or go for a walk and get some apples or pears or strawberries from the abundant farmlands of southern England.

The countryside was great compared to the city. You could get enough to live off by fossicking around. In my satchel I had underpants and socks, and cardboard for my shoes, because they weren't too crash hot in the bottom. This philosophy of being able to pick up and start again was born on the trains. I sometimes went three or four stops, got out, had a look and decided if I wanted to stay there a few days. There was a freedom in that.

Usually when I ran away, my aim was to fracture the relationship with the people I had been put with. When I couldn't take the abuse or violence that was going on, the SOP was to run away for at least twenty-four hours, just long enough to get them worried. It had to get to the point where they might have to call the cops, and they didn't want to do that, though some of them did.

Then there would be an instant handover because the people were freaking out about why I'd run away and whether I would talk, so everybody lied. We all lied. I didn't talk about all the bad things that might have happened because that would have been worse. There would be a huge investigation.

And they didn't berate me or say I was bad or evil. They just said, 'It's obvious he's not happy and it's probably best if he doesn't come back. If we take him he'll just run away again,' and I was then put back into the system.

I DID ENCOUNTER SOME good people in those years. Like the older couple who lived in a cottage where I had my own room and there were no other kids. The food was good and I could read my books.

But I don't think it was what they were expecting. Having a child around was problematic. They couldn't do things they normally would have done, because I was there. And sometimes I came home late because I had my paper round after school and they didn't like the fact I had missed tea.

The longest I stayed anywhere was six months, at a place called Boughton Monchelsea, which was a small village about thirty miles from Canterbury. It was a farming community and these people were farmers, Bert and Daisy, a brother and sister in their early seventies who had lived together in this cottage since their parents died. They had never married and had no children of their own.

Dentistry wasn't high on their agenda. I think they probably had three teeth between them. Bert was a combine-harvester driver and the gentlest of souls. They had a big garden which was overgrown with dandelions and nettles, and that was assigned to me to look after.

I would have stayed there because they liked me and I liked them. But when the end came, it wasn't because of some drama, for once. The deal had been explained clearly at the start.

They had a strict six-month limit so they could give lots of boys a chance. They believed it was their duty to take boys in and give them the experience of living on a farm in the hope it might encourage them to take up farming or at least get some direction.

Other stays were anywhere between three days and three months. I can't tell you how many families I stayed with, but I can tell you they covered a huge range of people. Occasionally there were people who were fostering because they thought it was their Christian obligation. Others thought it was their patriotic duty, because so many of us were homeless, directly or indirectly, as a result of the war.

A lot of the people had a fantasy of reliving life with their younger children who had grown up and left, or they were people who had lost kids and so they were trying to find a replacement. They became serial adopters — not necessarily because they disliked you but because there might be a better car just around the corner.

But usually they were the most dysfunctional examples of the human species you could get. As badly as I was treated, they often treated each other worse. It made it very hard for me later on even to think about having a relationship or children because of what I had seen happen. It was all the normal things plus the tragedies.

They weren't always my tragedies. One family I stayed with had a young son who owned an old Austin Somerset that he loved to drive at high speed. Once he agreed to pick me up from the next town and bring me home because it meant he could have a good long drive. I was waiting for him when I saw an ambulance tearing up the road away from me.

I waited an hour and he didn't show up. Then I saw his car being towed back the other way with the whole front caved in and an ominous hole in the driver's side windscreen.

I got on a bus and went home to find out he had been killed outright going around a bend.

This family had been fine to live with up to then. They were nice people. The boy had two older brothers who used to come to family dinners on Sundays.

But after the accident, the wife blamed me because he had been coming to get me when he was killed.

'I can't stand the sight of you,' she said to me one day. And so I had to go. It wasn't my fault and it wasn't even theirs; it was circumstance, but it reinforced my feeling that people could not be trusted.

And because the system was full of kids needing homes, when you left under circumstances like that, you ended up in a halfway house before they found a billet for you. That was rough, but once I got characterised as a problem kid there was no going back.

I THINK I WAS ALWAYS different, even down to little things. In the orphanages, for instance, you had to eat quickly because the servings weren't big and if someone else finished their meal they would simply take yours. I hated all of that. I liked things to be nice, and I don't know where that came from. Knife and fork lined up. Everything tidy. Most of the people around me had no idea life could be nice. But I had gone off on my walks and looked through the window of Claridge's and seen how nice life could be. I didn't want to go in there because it looked terrifying — but it was beautiful too.

One of the few friends I made in all those years, when I was twelve, was a boy my age called Graeme. He and I had a connection because he arrived with a whole lot of books. I was drawing as well, copying pictures, and he had a lot of Roy

Rogers comics that I loved.

He was very intelligent and we had proper conversations about life and what our aspirations were. That sort of bond was rare.

But Graeme was also very vulnerable. He was big for his age and a very good-looking boy with a crop of blond hair and very pale, luminescent skin. He was a quiet, gentle boy and just the sort paedophiles find really attractive.

One of our caregivers became obsessed with him and sodomised him frequently in the dormitory. His bed was next to mine, and some nights in the half-light, when this was going on, I looked across and Graeme was looking at me and I was looking at him, and this guy was looking at me too, and I was a victim of the same situation because he was getting off on me being part of the whole thing. Paedophiles like that want you to have eye contact so they know that they're in control.

Eventually I spoke out, prompted I think by my earlier experiences of violence and injustice.

I convinced Graeme that we should go to the head administrator and tell him what was happening. We told him our story and he agreed to follow up but advised that the teacher was well respected and a good teacher, which he was, and advised that he was confident that no further 'incidents' would take place and it would be best not to mention this again.

But like so many things, it was a political decision. I realised later the immorality of that: I had gone to somebody in trust to try to stop something bad happening, and I got a political response.

And, of course, this man felt rejected because his affection for Graeme was genuine. He had just taken it to that next level. So he felt betrayed and he took that out on the boy. And one day it got too much and Graeme went into the changing rooms and hanged himself.

It was the 5th of May, whatever year it was that I was twelve and a half. I remember the date because on the 6th of May I ran away for the last time.

THREE

Under the bridge

I lived under a railway bridge for the next eight months. I didn't run away because I was frightened that Graeme's abuser would turn his attention to me; I had simply had enough. Yet again, I felt betrayed by the people who were supposed to be looking after me, and I decided the best thing I could do was make my own way in the world.

I believed I'd kill somebody rather than go back to that life. I knew I was running away forever and I knew that it was doable. I'd been planning it, collecting bits of stuff for my big escape and practising jumping out windows. I was an expert on train timetables and had them in my satchel for all the trains. I knew how to run across tracks and hop on another train to go to another place.

I knew I had to find somewhere permanent to live. I had this grandiose idea that London was the place to start a new life and reinvent myself. London was exciting. People in London lived those nice lives I had seen through the window of Claridge's. My suitcase was pretty much packed and ready to rock and roll at any time. I had my school jacket, which was dirty because I couldn't wash it, and I had my tie. But a school jacket was a killer as well, because it got you into places. I'd learnt that if you wanted to get stale buns or a cup of tea and sit in the warm lobby of a smart hotel then you had to look the part.

I spent the first week, while I was looking for somewhere to sleep, travelling up and down on the trains. I still keep an eye out for likely places to sleep out, even today, perhaps driving through Newton Gully near my home in Auckland. I wasn't in a hurry when I first ran away because it was the middle of summer and I could sleep on a bench for a few nights.

In London all the safe and warm places were taken by professional hobos who were determined to protect their patch, especially from a thirteen-year-old. I kept getting on the train and off again and walking around different areas, hoping to find somewhere secure and sheltered.

I also thought of going down to Canterbury, where I had lived with my parents and gone to primary school. There was a railway bridge I knew of there that looked like a good position, but it was often frequented by kids walking up the railway line. I realised that the smaller the location was, the more visible I was. In the provinces I would be noticed, yet on the streets of London I would get the crap beaten out of me.

Eventually I came to Finsbury Park Railway Station in north London. I walked a few clicks up the line and there was an over-bridge for a small roadway and a passageway for pedestrians that led across to the park itself, which is a huge, beautiful space with lovely big oak trees. It was a classic, old-fashioned Victorian park that fell into neglect in the seventies. I was probably one of the vagrants who began its decline.

The space under the bridge was ideal as a shelter for me because there were lots of people walking overhead but nobody knew how to climb down and get to my spot. Coming from the other direction, you had to be very fit to make the ascent. You couldn't just walk up. The main security feature was the location.

I decided to get set up there. I didn't want anyone to know I was living there. I was secure but I had a residue of fear after being at other people's mercy for so long, and I behaved accordingly. Whenever I went down the embankment to get up on the railway bridge, I took a different path so a track didn't get worn into the ground. And I never climbed down from the parapet onto the railway line if there was a train coming. I made sure that nobody could discover me. I became an expert at that so I could have a free life.

For my home, I found an old aluminium glasshouse frame from the back of an allotment and used wire to fix some cardboard and black polythene around it to act as a windbreaker. That wasn't a total success to begin with because when a train came through it created a vortex that swept everything away that wasn't bolted down. If you left a book out, it went flying down the line. I had to reinforce everything with chicken wire.

The covering was blackout gear that also stopped the light from my torch being seen from outside. I didn't want it seeping out to let anyone know I was up there. I fastened everything up, then slipped out to make sure not a glimmer could be seen.

Occasionally, railway workers came down the track to do

inspections. I sat and waited and listened as they passed by on the lines below.

As a routine, it wasn't that different from coming home to my mother's house and hiding up in the attic with my torch and books to get away from the catastrophe going on downstairs. It was much scarier sleeping in an orphanage than outside under a bridge.

I went looking for a Primus stove to cook on, but they were far too expensive. Instead I went to a second-hand shop and found an old brass, blowtorch-style paint stripper. But the rubber washer that pressurised the chamber work was buggered, so it was useless. Not to be beaten, I managed to take a bit of leather off the lining of one of my shoes and used that as a piston seal. And that meant that I could take a can of beans, put it on a stone and put the blowtorch on it and heat it up for tea at night. It probably worked much better than the gas ring, which just heats from the low end. It worked on everything except milk, which tended to explode or burn. With my paint stripper I could have made crème brûlée — and probably did a few times without knowing it.

Over time I made the place a home; I had some plastic plates and a sleeping bag. All the money I earned from my paper rounds — I had one in the morning and one at night all through this period — was spent getting myself set up. They provided me with enough to live on during this time.

I kept empty cans and converted them for cooking equipment by banging in holes with my trusty knife and attaching bits of wire to make handles. I got posters of planes — bombers and Spitfires — that I put up. One very important item was a truckload of cardboard. I had four or five layers of that underneath me because it's the best insulator. That took a long time to organise.

The centre of London, where the train lines converged, was no use because it was desolate and the only businesses were places that operated on a cash-only basis. I needed someone selling refrigerators, for the big boxes. The Finsbury Park area wasn't particularly plush either, so I had to go to the provinces and do some foraging.

I found the boxes but had a struggle getting them home. I had to fold them up to get them on the train, and I could only get them through one at a time, piling them up on the platform. When my train arrived, the moment the door opened I rushed to throw the boxes on and jump on behind. At the other end I did the same thing in reverse.

But for the first time in my life I had found a piece of magic — a home, a place I felt safe. I wanted to hold on to it, so I put some effort into making it right. I could scramble up the bank from my shelter and I had a view of the park with its lake in the middle.

And in the eight months I stayed, no one ever found out I was there. I was incredibly diligent about not leaving a footprint to be discovered. I collected up all my rubbish and took it in bags to dump at the station. I even used to worry about smells when I was cooking, in case someone noticed them and got suspicious.

And I am sure no one ever came looking for me. There were such big holes in the system that if you were smart it was easy to slip through them. For a start, if I didn't turn up at school, and anyone noticed, where would they have sent a note? The records were probably three foster homes behind me. No one from a home where I was no longer living had any interest in my welfare. The classes were big and teachers were only barely aware of who was in them, so they wouldn't ask questions. I didn't have any friends of the sort who would miss me.

I had a choice about attending school. I could still have lived under the bridge and gone to lessons every day, but I didn't think I would learn much I needed to know. Instead, as Noel Coward once said: 'At the age of fourteen I left school and commenced my education.'

I did go to school occasionally. Sometimes I went to lessons to see what was going on. I also got bored from time to time and went to remind myself that I was better off under the bridge by seeing how awful school was. Once I went when assembly was on. I opened the hall doors and heard 1500 kids singing something irrelevant — almost certainly 'All Things Bright and Beautiful' — and shut the door and quietly walked away.

THE OTHER IMPORTANT STRATEGY to avoid being caught was to keep moving. I knew with absolute conviction that if I kept going back to the same place I would get found out. If I went to the same coffee bar every day, people there would realise I wasn't going to school and they might tell somebody.

Occasionally, when I was reading a book in a tea shop someone asked, 'Shouldn't you be at school?'

'I'm planning for an exam and they're giving me time off as long as I do this, because this is better for me,' was my SOP stock answer. I stayed in tea shops reading, and as long as I bought a tea every couple of hours it was fine.

If I had a long-term plan at that stage, it was that when I was the legal age I would join the army. I never thought about what I was going to do for the three and a half years in between.

Also, I had that awareness of a better kind of life which included the Woman in the White Dress. That vision just kept getting clearer, even though it was so far from becoming a reality. The woman would come down to the stream in the park and I would help her over that log in the stream. I knew exactly how

I would feel, even then. And when I finally met Anna, that's exactly how I did feel.

But at the same time, I was a thirteen-year-old boy relishing some freedom and independence. I 'borrowed' car magazines from the newsagent I was delivering papers for and fantasised about having a flash car as much as I did about the Woman in the White Dress. I tore out pictures of cars and put them up around the walls of my shelter. They turned out to be much easier to acquire than the woman.

I was free, happy and at peace living under the bridge. It was the freedom of not being told what to do. Up to then everything in my life had been institutionalised, to the point of being told when to go to the toilet in some cases. I got to choose not only when but where I went to the toilet, and sometimes I went to an expensive hotel and sat reading in their lobby before I used their facilities. On those occasions, if anyone asked, I was waiting for my aunty to take me to the doctor.

I may not have been cooking gourmet feasts, but I liked the simplicity of buying food to make a meal and cooking it when I wanted to and eating it when I wanted to. It was hardly ever worse than what I had been served up in orphanages.

The happiest time of all was Sunday morning. Just having a lie-in was a luxury after living in places where every morning somebody came in and made me get up at the same time as a crowd of other boys to shower together and line up together to be inspected with another person pulling your socks up and straightening your shoelaces. Nothing in those places was mine. In my Finsbury Park empire, everything was mine — the pictures of cars and planes and the balsawood models, my books and assorted fruit winegums. Lovely.

When I got up on Sunday — late — sometimes I caught the

train to Victoria Station and went to a café to have a cup of tea before having a spin around the science museum. Often I was following up on something I had read and trying to get a better understanding of it. Later, back at the park, I sat in the rotunda and watched the people go by. Or I lay under a tree, reading a book and scribbling.

I treated myself to fish and chips and sometimes managed to score a beer from the pub. I didn't like beer, but I liked the idea of being able to have it.

The single biggest difference from my old life was that I was no longer afraid. I didn't spend my days worrying about what someone might do or say. It was my life and nobody was going to jump into bed with me or smack me over the head.

I was like a king because the day was mine. I could do anything, knowing that when night came I had somewhere safe to sleep and would not go to bed hungry.

My other refuge at this time was the public library system. I spent days and sometimes nights in public libraries, gaining an education.

Of course, having no fixed address or paperwork, I couldn't get a library card, so I had to do all my reading in the libraries themselves. And that meant I had to move from library to library so as not to arouse suspicion from the regulars.

The regulars were that other group of people who spend a lot of time in libraries: old-age pensioners who appreciate the free heating and probably also have no one else at home to keep them company.

I got used to seeing an old man opposite me with a Gannex raincoat and cap and smelling of pipe smoke. There was one in any library you went to.

'What are you doing here?' The question always came, sooner

or later. I used one of my stock excuses. I think they were probably more interested in having a chat than catching me out. They were the only people who asked.

I developed a system of piling up books in front of me like a barricade to hide behind. I could also use it to quietly slip a few books into my satchel to take home without anyone seeing.

Inevitably, one night as I was leaving, one of the librarians busted me. She was impressed by the standard of books I was nicking.

'I'm going to give you your own library card,' she said, and she made one up and gave it to me. It was one of the nicest things anyone had done for me.

One of my favourite things to sit down with and get lost in was the *Encyclopaedia Britannica*; it was one publication I could be sure of finding, no matter what library I was in.

I think it played a large part in making me interested in the world beyond my own little part of it. It was both a magazine, full of all sorts of different things, and a Rosetta Stone, something that helped me make sense of what was going on. I dipped into it, found something that fascinated me and then followed up on that line of inquiry in the library proper. I could use it to find out about something I was interested in, or I could use it to find something to be interested in, by opening a page at random and reading what was there.

At school I had been exposed to Charles Dickens and Geoffrey Chaucer. Having spent those years in Canterbury, I was naturally intrigued by Chaucer's *Canterbury Tales* — stories told by pilgrims making the journey to that city, which I saw as a collection of journals by a group of travellers. It was like a documentary covering the history and anthropology of that time and place.

I also learnt to love language used well. *Treasure Island*, which

I had read years before, had been a turning point, because it was a long novel, and it transported me away from everything that was bad in my life at the time. So I looked for other adventures, like *Huckleberry Finn*, and *The Man in the Iron Mask*. I read everything I could get my hands on.

Books served other purposes besides escapism. They were my teachers, and my friends. But eventually I got bored with adventure stories and started to get more interested in the way things worked. I started with the basics and worked out how the library cataloguing system worked, so I could use it to find out just about anything I wanted to know. And not just how things worked, but how people worked too. Once I discovered one of Leonardo da Vinci's inventions in a book and I wanted to learn about the physics behind it so went and researched leverage.

I was looking for answers to all sorts of questions, from: 'Why was my mum like that?' to much bigger questions about how the systems I had been through had come to be that way, and what was likely to happen in the future. Those questions have followed me down the years.

Time goes very quickly if you're absorbed in books that deeply. As well as the libraries I also spent a lot of time at the Tate Gallery. Sometimes I stayed looking at the same painting for ages. That started me learning about painting techniques. For instance, when I painted the sea I used a product called Miskit to mask where I wanted the wave caps to be. Then I did a wash across and took the Miskit off to leave the white behind. I read somewhere that Turner got into trouble when he did a painting of a stormy sea and used a scalpel to scrape away paint and leave white wave caps behind. This was not regarded as painting. I read about this and was able to go and track down the painting, see for myself what he had done and take home a lesson for my own painting.

I spent a lot of time teaching myself how to paint. There was a horse period, where I struggled and struggled to get the horse to look like a horse. The first one I did had the legs facing in the wrong direction, because I did it from memory. So I got pictures of horses and copied them until I got it right. Doing that led me on to studying human anatomy — how the muscles worked and the body was put together. Which led on to exploring how internal organs worked.

I had always been one to follow a subject as far as I could. Even at school, the things I remembered were those bits of the maths curriculum or the English curriculum which joined the dots between things I already knew.

I also found many of my heroes at this time. What I loved most — my great escape — was reading about people who had made a success of their lives.

Reading Chaucer, I learnt that his work had been printed by William Caxton, the first English printer. So I started investigating and found out Caxton was a bit like me, in that he had no parents to speak of. And that was very powerful, because it made me think: maybe I can have as much impact as Caxton. I didn't have any idea how, back then, though I do now.

As I read on I learnt that Caxton didn't have a master plan. He had been a milliner, was travelling around Europe and had seen a printing press in Bruges and realised the potential.

For me, following trails like that was early training in applied science — one thing led naturally to another, but you also had to remember how each element related at each step of the way. I was learning that I had a good analytical brain.

Everything connected up for me. For instance, I had read lots of Greek legends, which were like the best adventure stories, really, with pictures of gods and giants and spears and horses. And that led me to study what makes people tick, because all those stories were about the human condition — betrayal, trust, love and hate.

And that connected with my admiration for René Descartes, which came about in the first place because I enjoyed being transported back to his place and time when I read about him.

He was trying to understand the same things as me. He had some wonderful lines. He was once in a big battle and said, 'Being away from the front and having no female companions to worry about or no war to fight, it occurred to me that I'd have time to think.' And he started to rationalise everything and eventually got to 'I think, therefore I am', which he said was the first thing we could really be certain of. That struck a chord. Under the railway bridge, I was facing the real deal of how to go on staying alive, and I was face to face with my own existence and my control over it.

Descartes was a brilliant mathematician too, and for me philosophy was just as practical as learning how to fix a car. I learnt how mathematics was applied to paintings and how the scale of things in them could be perfect. I took that knowledge to the Tate Gallery and applied it to the pictures I saw there.

The knowledge I was acquiring under the bridge was applied science. At school I had been learning algebra and other things that I couldn't see a practical place for in the scheme of life.

I was starting to develop a scientist's outlook: if you know enough stuff you can make the connections between things that people find difficult. The ability to do that started when I went off on my own and tried to work things out while my school friends were playing together, having gangs and being taught an arcane curriculum. That's how I worked out so early that if I put on a tie and jacket, I could live under a railway bridge but still get into the best hotels and sit in their lobbies and read books.

Keeping to my practical path, I kept up the science experiments. I eventually rigged up a lighting system based on a dynamo. I could generate and store electricity in six-volt motorcycle batteries, which was a lot cheaper than using torch batteries.

I was probably one of the first people in the world to make an electric drill out of a DC motor. I was playing around along those lines. I got a drill to work. I didn't have the gearing and casing to give it any real torque but I was playing with the concept. It was a work in progress but nothing ever came of it. Somebody thought of the same thing later on and made it all work.

It's harder to teach yourself science than history or literature. When you first pick up a book on chemistry, unless you've had some basic training, it's incomprehensible. But my early explorations in science led me down more adventurous, imaginative pathways.

I looked at the Industrial Revolution, and how it used science and technology to change society. By just looking a little more closely I was soon investigating things like the Solvay process, which revolutionised the production of sodium bicarbonate, which meant that the washing industry could get going. I was captivated to see how one thing led to another.

BY NOW I WAS only going to school when I needed a shower. In summer it was fine. About 800 metres from my shelter was a waterway where I could go for a swim, and there was a little hut with a tap on the side of it, about 50 metres up the railway line, so I went there and had a wipe under the arms regularly.

But there were mundane parts to life under the bridge —

drying myself with a small towel and seeing skid marks on my underpants and thinking I had to go and wash them. I had moments of self-realisation when I woke up and I smelt. I thought: 'I'll have to go down to the school and have a real shower instead of an underarm wipe.'

As it got colder, I cleaned myself up in the toilets on the train. They were brilliant because they had hot running water.

But schools had showers and nobody noticed one small boy going in to use them when the more basic ablutions weren't enough. I sometimes turned up at lunchtime for a free feed if I felt like a change. It only worked when I knew the class schedules, so that I could make sure I went in when no one from my class who knew me would be there.

I could also afford to use a public laundry when my clothes really needed to be done. I took them in there at the start of my paper round and picked them up again at the end.

I still had my grey clothes and brown shoes and uniform jacket and school tie. But I needed two sets of clothes to function, not just for hygiene but also from a psychological perspective. Normally I wanted to fit in, and that's why I wore the tie and tried not to be noticed. Ironically, there was that other part of me that wanted to be a peacock, and when I had finally made it, years later, I took every opportunity to stand out. I reinvented myself in the flower-power years. It was fun. The Beatles were around and Hendrix was on the radio — it was a beautiful time to be an adolescent and I was the man.

For now, however, I needed a set of clothes that were not school uniform. I needed something a little more fashionable than grey, grey, grey and brown. I was coming into puberty and, although the Beatles were still a little way off, drainpipe trousers and thin lapels were in. I went to the local haberdashery shop and got double-sided, iron-on tape which you could use to alter clothes if you couldn't sew well.

Armed with that, I adapted one of my orphanage jackets — I made it shorter, and made cuffs and lapels with the iron-on tape. I made myself look cool. Then I bought some cotton and thread and hand-sewed the pants to make them narrower and put double-sided tape on to keep them from fraying. I was cool. I had never had any good clothes but I always wanted them.

I could afford all this because of the paper run, which was a great gig. I got up at 4.30 and the trains started running at five. The newsagent and his wife used to cook me breakfast every morning. They had no idea where I was living. Or if they did they decided not to say anything. After about six months they were like a little mini-family, but everything was straight-up because I was also doing a good job for them and I was one of the more reliable kids, so it was a good commercial relationship where they paid me every day in cash. They were not trying to step outside that arrangement and give me some false hope about a rosy family future. After the evening run I had dinner out of a can, or sometimes just a drink of milk if I'd had something proper to eat during the day. Then it was bedtime — but with *me* deciding when the light went out. To snuggle down in safety was absolute bliss.

That was the extent of my regular human contact in those eight months: the newsagent and his wife, the guy at the laundry and the guys at the pub next door, plus the boys who did the round, a few librarians and occasionally people at school if I popped in. As to any sense of loneliness — for a start I wasn't, and beyond that, the sense of freedom and the relief of not being institutionalised outweighed any downside. I loved my own company and began to feel happy.

These were early entrepreneurial exercises for me too. I came in early to do the round mark-up for the other boys' delivery and organise the piles of publications and put them together for their runs as well as my own. One bonus there was that there was the man at number 27 who used to get *Playboy* delivered — I liked having a read of that.

One boy was my contractor and was renting a bike from me. I had started a bike-renting business while I was still at school, using bikes I put together from bits I found at the tip. I needed to get them back for the paper round because a friend of one of the boys wanted to do a round but didn't have a bike of his own. I said I would supply one for a percentage of his round. I couldn't afford to take the bikes on the train, because they were charged as freight. So I had to catch the train to get them one at a time and ride them back to Finsbury Park, a distance of about 100 kilometres.

There was a motorway for the route, but you couldn't take a bike on it, so I had to go the long way. I loved riding and stopping on the country roads at orchards for something to eat, or sitting by the side of the road and relaxing when I wanted to.

On one trip the chain broke and I didn't have anything to repair it with, so I had to push the bike. Finally, I got to this big hill and the pedals kept rotating and hitting my ankles. It was getting worse and worse and I was tired, and I thought, 'At least it's not raining,' which was when the clouds opened up on a biblical scale. I was halfway up the hill, soaked to the skin and laughing my head off, and still laughing when I got to the next village and was able to borrow some pliers and a bit of wire to fix it.

I was never in any danger on those adventures, and seldom had to worry in the park in the daytime. At night, away from my shelter, it filled up with alcoholics, druggies and people wanting to have a quick shag. I stayed away at night.

I always tried to stay away from the main traffic areas during the day too, so I could settle down and be undisturbed. But if you followed the sun to stay warm, you might end up in the main traffic area and you'd get everybody ranging from the paedophile coming to try and get you, to the old people who were concerned about a schoolboy sitting under a tree in the middle of the day.

Paedophiles were a problem when I sat outside to read in summer. Men walked by and said hello. If you answered them, they thought they had you and stopped to try to talk to you. I pulled out my knife and did my little psycho act and they kept going. In a way, I'm lucky they were paedophiles — anyone else would have gone to the police and reported a schoolkid sitting in the park waving a knife at strangers. But that never happened.

ONCE WINTER CAME, it wasn't easy to fill time and it was a lot less comfortable. There was no way you could sit underneath that railway bridge in the cold, so I rode up and down on the train to the southern coast all day. Those rides were luxurious. I found my own compartment with brilliant heating, put my feet up and got stuck into a book. But the trains stopped running about midnight. I had to make sure I got back to the park in time or I had to sleep rough in a station.

Winter also made the climb up to my shelter difficult because the stones I normally used to grip to climb up became slippery. In the end I rigged up a rope with knots to hold on to.

I tied a piece of fishing nylon around the bottom bit and, when I wasn't using it, I'd throw the whole rope up the top and put the nylon tracer in the cracks of the walls, so you couldn't see it.

Some mornings I woke up with the top of my sleeping bag

frozen white. My SOP at bedtime was to sleep in a tracksuit with newspapers around my legs and up my thighs for insulation.

I didn't want to get out of bed but I had to because I had the paper round. After that I often went back to bed with a book, because I was too cold or tired to go to the library or even ride the trains.

One day I slipped coming down the parapet and cut myself and it got infected. I had already been sick from something I had eaten and the cold weather made everything worse. The infection turned to blood poisoning, and that was my lowest moment. I thought, 'If I die now, nobody will know. Not a single person on this planet will know that I'm dead.' I had chilblains, but somehow I managed to get on a train to get warm. I got so warm I fell asleep. And instead of getting off before the last train, I was still there when the guards came around to inspect the carriages before they put them into the sidings.

They found me and called the cops. I had my school uniform on and my school hymn book in my backpack. So it wasn't hard for the police to work out where I was supposed to be. They called up the school, and by the time I woke up in hospital there was the usual friendly-faced social worker sitting next to me.

By some miracle, however, I wasn't sent back to one of the old institutions. By some act of fate I came to the attention of Jack Wise.

FOUR

Pygmalion

I never saw my shelter again. And I never once thought of going back to collect my things. I left that part of my life behind and looked towards the future.

I was still in hospital when Jack Wise came to see me. He was the gardening teacher at school and had been there when the cops rang to say I had been found. He was also a do-gooder in the right sense — he spent his weekends visiting prisoners in jail who had no one else to take an interest in them. Apart from that, I never knew much about his personal life. I think he may have had a son who turned out badly and that may have been what motivated his social philanthropy. He also wore some badges which were probably from service clubs, but I never found out. I was still more interested in getting people to love me than in loving people myself.

Jack jumped on a train and came to meet me. He was the image of a gardener with his big brown boots, baggy cord trousers and baggy jacket. He had a fag on the go and he looked like he could mug you in a dark alley.

'I've got this class, 4RH, that I'm starting,' he said. 'You've got two choices. You come in the class or we'll put you in a bloody borstal. It's your choice, a one-time offer expiring now. And you have to live where I tell you to live and like it. If you do that, then I guarantee you'll get a decent education out of what I'm going to teach you.'

4RH stood for rural horticulture. I would have done it even without the threat of borstal because I liked Jack. There was something about him that was different.

He found me a home which turned out to be the nicest digs I ever had. The house belonged to a spinster, Annie Brown, who had spent her whole life looking after her mother. She was now in her fifties and had a boarder, Mr McDonald, who was in his eighties, sported a waxed handlebar moustache and had lived there for twenty years. Jack arranged for them to take me in and we formed this odd family unit.

Really we were more like flatmates. The man cooked himself breakfast every morning and I was struck by the way he put pepper on everything. Then he joined his mates and spent the day sitting on a bench watching the world go by. The woman went off every day too and did her thing. And I just slipped in alongside them. Occasionally I had meals with them, but I could come and go as I pleased and nobody minded. I had the same freedom as under the bridge but a lot more comfort and security.

All I owned was the clothes I had been wearing when I was found. Jack arranged some more for me through the army and navy relief society, but they were the same old grey everything I had before. I got some more double-sided tape and had a go at smartening them up.

Later, instead of keeping the money she got for taking me in, which included a clothing allowance, and doling it out — or using it to buy things for herself — the woman put it on the table and said: 'That's yours. Go and buy yourself some proper clothes.'

I loved Jack because he took an interest in me and I wanted to please him. I worked hard academically and took a lot of O levels to show that his faith had not been misplaced. I threw myself into academic work, and he is the only teacher I ever did that for.

I struggled a little with the fact that in the time between Jack finding me and my starting at 4RH he went from being a friend to being a teacher. That was strange because he had personalised the relationship. But it was just the way he was — the message being that I had to make my own way. I thought I was special to him because of the interest he had taken in me, but he only did that because that was what he did. It wouldn't have mattered who I was or what I was like, he would have done the same.

Jack was a great teacher. The new class was more practical and science-based than other gardening courses. He talked about the history and chemistry behind agriculture. We learnt about Jethro Tull and the invention of the plough and hydroponics (growing plants in water) early on. We spent some of our time in the classroom but the rest of it was learning how to drive a tractor and look after pigs and grow things in our allotments. We also ran a chicken farm, pushing hens' insides back in after they had prolapsed and killing them when the time came.

We went on trips to see how farms worked, how a milk factory was run, and once to Dagenham to see how cars were made. His philosophy was that we needed to be educated about the world at large and not just about 'subjects'. In fact, the course did not even give you an official qualification. Jack's aim was to prepare the lads for what they were destined to end up doing, which was being a farm worker in most cases.

Our classroom was stupendous. It was a huge barn with benches in the stalls to serve as desks. We sat side-saddle to watch Jack and the blackboard at the far end. In the middle of the room was a massive vintage TVO Massey Ferguson tractor that he had scored from somebody. There were two big doors but above one was a slot that had been cut out so the chimney of the tractor could fit through. Outside we had all the chickens and pigs and the allotments that we were running. It was fun, dynamic and interesting.

Something that was no different from my old school days was the amount of bullying that went on. But I was different now. I didn't defend myself, because if I had, Jack would not have been happy. He would have been horrified that I was carrying a weapon. I threw my knife away and tried to avoid trouble.

Behind the bullying was a perception that I was somehow Jack's favourite — even though I wasn't feeling that way at all.

'You're the fucking teacher's pet,' one of the bullies said once when I had been sent to the shops to buy some hardware, which was seen as a treat.

'Jack's just sending me down to get the stuff,' I explained, 'and I'm just going to get the stuff.'

I could have taken this guy easily, but being caught fighting would have been letting Jack down. So I took the hiding, went to the shop and brought the things back to Jack, who could see I had been in a stoush.

'What happened to you?' he asked.

'Nothing.'

MY FIRST RETAIL entrepreneurial stirrings occurred around this time. With my paper rounds and the bike hire I had always been a commercial animal. But I had never had so much access to produce before. We grew a lot of things that were usually sold to the teachers.

Things were not set up commercially, but when I looked after the chickens on the weekend I knocked off a few eggs and set up shop on the side of the road with a beautiful handwritten sign: 'Fresh Organic Eggs'.

I got caught, of course.

'The hens seem to be laying very regularly,' Jack told the class one day as he went through the records we kept, 'except when Ray Avery is looking after them, when the yield goes down 25 per cent. I didn't understand this anomaly until last weekend when I was out driving past the school and saw Ray Avery beside the road selling eggs. I think he's come up with a brilliant idea, and because he's so good at it, I'm going to make him man the stall for nothing for the next six months.'

I had another casual job at the same time in a fish-and-chip shop. My task was to chop up the peeled potatoes into chips. Keeping up with production on a Friday night when the pubs closed was madness.

We grew potatoes at the school, so I came up with the idea of chopping lots of them into chips in advance. I thought it had the makings of a fine business.

So I got all the potatoes at school, washed them and put them through a potato peeler borrowed from the shop. Then I got my schoolmates to come in early one morning before anyone else was there, and we chopped them up into chips and put them into plastic bags and I took them to the shop where I worked.

'Here's all your bags of chips,' I said. 'We can do this for you and for a good price. You don't even have to go to the market to buy the potatoes; we'll just deliver you the chips.'

'Great,' he said.

We had just one customer and we thought we were making a fortune. It was about £10. Then I got ambitious and decided to scale things up. I went to other chip shops and offered them our pre-prepared chips. We delivered bags and bags of them. It worked for about ten days, until the potatoes started to go brown, which was making the chips go brown.

So I went to the library and read up about oxidation. I was learning. Every wrong answer was really just something directing me to the right answer.

We liberated a nitrogen cylinder from the physics lab and we were back in business. With the nitrogen treatment the potatoes kept for months in the fridge. That business grew to the point that I was able to sell it.

So my first proper business was a combination of gardening that depended on applied science and technology.

Jack was in tune with the business side of things. He saw it as a different kind of opportunity he could provide for us. Another early commercial endeavour of mine was his idea.

'Look,' he said to me one day, 'I've got a lot of friends who want to get their gardens sorted out. I thought you might be able to get a few of the lads together and we'll start a landscaping operation. You can have all the money but you've got to do it bloody right because my reputation's on the line.'

I organised the guys into groups and did the landscape designs myself — this shrub here, a trellis there, a path here. The lads got paid a pittance and now a fourteen-year-old was turning up at people's houses, showing them designs and telling them the best plants to use. None of it would have happened if Jack hadn't shown me the opportunities.

When the time came to leave 4RH in 1962, Jack helped me get

a job as a technician at Wye College, an agricultural institution in Kent. I had great experience and a lot of knowledge, but I had no proper qualifications so they were taking me on his recommendation.

I had learnt how to be a good student in 4RH. At Wye I was to learn how to be a good person.

THE FIRST TIME I turned up there I went to the wrong place. I bowled up to the front entrance of a fifteenth-century building. I walked through the huge arch and into the quadrangle.

Institutions like Wye don't have a reception area — everybody knows where they are going. I wandered around for ages but could not find anything that looked like a research centre to me.

I was convinced I had come to the wrong place and was ready to walk away when I found someone who was able to show me where to go.

It was another one of those moments in which my life got turned around and pointed in a new direction. The men I met here were the making of me in so many ways.

Firstly, they were all dressed in white coats, and until that time the only person I'd ever seen in a lab coat was a doctor. These were all career scientists. They explained that they did plant substance analysis and one asked me if I had studied botany.

'I know about hydroponics,' I said.

'That's a good start,' he said. And he patted me on the head.

The agricultural research centre was in a collection of buildings some distance from the romantic old one I had first gone to. And beyond it were hundreds of acres of glasshouses and other facilities.

The men I worked with were lecturers at the college who also did government-funded fundamental research, which is what I was there to help them with.

Under their white coats they wore three-piece suits with cufflinks and university college ties. Some wore aftershave, some smoked pipes or cigarettes from silver cases and many smelt of tobacco. When they came to work in the morning they shook each other's hands, and when they went home in the evening, they shook hands again. Over their coffee they had conversations about art and politics. I loved hearing them talk about Plato and poetry and history. I was enchanted. I had never met anyone like these men. Not only were they intelligent, they were the first truly caring people I had ever met *en masse*. Before this, the caring people had been the exceptions like Bert and Daisy, the brother and sister who had taken me in for a while, or Jack.

Oddly, I felt they were like me, even though we were so different. They were like the books I loved to read, except they were real live people. So, although they were outside my direct experience, everything about them was strangely familiar.

Many of them had served in the war, which was still fresh in their memories a decade and a half on. There was one who had been a classic fighter pilot with his little quiff of hair and square jaw. He had flown numerous sorties where he had gone out and could easily have been killed, and he had coped with that by distancing himself emotionally from it.

I took comfort from that because, although I had been involved in violence, it was nothing like his experience of people shooting at you and having friends die. I felt less alone hearing about that sort of experience.

Many of them didn't need to work for the money. They had boats and big houses and plenty of disposable income. They were here because they were interested in science. They were true academics, and as a result of my time there I've always been drawn to academia.

The research was reasonably mediocre, to be honest. There were about twenty of them all up and although one professor was a world expert on plant growth substances, it was a small talent pool.

I was also exposed for the first time to people from another culture. Wye had received money from the United Arab Emirates and people from there were at the college.

But they were interested in having a nice life — the one on the other side of the Claridge's window. That was what I was most attracted to at Wye and that was what I learnt most about during my time there.

I had bought a motorbike and one day my boss asked to have a look at it. Somehow I must have charmed or intrigued him because at the end he invited me to lunch with the professors. Wye was a live-in college with its own chefs and kitchens, but they didn't care for what came out of there. They had their own waiter and developed relationships with local suppliers. An informal lunch arrangement had developed whereby people ate away from the canteen and brought along better food than the college supplied. Often I was sent to buy it and there was never lunch without some wine.

And I think, as much as they had been a revelation to me, I was a revelation to them. Their lives had been sheltered. They came from good families, had gone to Eton, Oxford and Cambridge. I skipped over the worst things that had happened long ago, and I never told them about that, but they had never met, let alone been intimately involved with, anyone from my world.

I must have told some good anecdotes and got a few laughs because they decided to take me on. They realised I knew nothing about food or wine or how to dress properly, which were things that were terribly important to them because they made life pleasant. Of course, I also made sure they knew I was well read and intelligent, so they thought it was worth putting the effort into my transformation.

'We can't have you going through life like that, young Ray,' was the general attitude.

FIRST WERE THE MUSHROOMS.

'Would you like some mushrooms, young Ray?' asked a professor who was supervising, frying some up for lunch.

I had never eaten or been offered a mushroom.

'No,' I said. 'I don't like them. To be honest, I've never seen one before and they look all greasy and terrible.'

'Good Lord,' he said. 'Then these will be not only the best mushrooms you have ever eaten but also the first.'

I had had fish paste before, but never pâté. Or artichokes. There were so many things I ate for the first time at work with the professors.

In the summer, particularly, everything was abandoned to go and sit outdoors in one of the quadrangles, taking some tables and chairs out or just putting a blanket down. Those lunches went on for maybe two hours. And one of the reasons was that they were using that time to teach me, and they loved it.

Some of it was pure *Darling Buds of May*. We had our own cornfields and when we needed wheat for experiments we went out and cut it with little hand scythes. For the first time, I saw the professors take off their jackets and waistcoats and roll up their sleeves. We cut the straw and hay and at the end, as if by magic, women appeared with baskets and hampers and we had a huge picnic.

It was just beautiful and the complete antithesis of life on the streets. I lay on a bale of wheat in the sun thinking, 'This is paradise. Life is never going to be any better than this.' And it was probably true, but this was because I had no responsibilities, and that could not last forever.

If they had finished their teaching duties they often skipped the research in favour of a game of tennis on the college courts. I didn't have anything to do so I went to watch.

'Give Ray a bit of a knock-around,' my boss said one day, and that's how I learnt to play tennis. And bridge. And chess.

Their children came in to meet them occasionally and it was like something from a movie in my eyes. I had never seen families that actually loved each other and weren't dysfunctional but really caring and appreciative.

Their method of educating me was often scientific and experimental.

'Young Ray, you can't go through life without knowing how to order a decent bottle of wine.' And then they'd send me down to the shop to buy stuff and come back and we'd have lunch and taste it.

'Here is some brie, young Ray, which is different from the brie you had yesterday. This one is from the South of France, and you'll notice a little bit more rigid and turgid than the other one, but we want you to pick one of these three wines that you think would go with this, Ray. One of them is an absolutely perfect combination. The other two I wouldn't recommend. I want you to tell me which one.'

And they kept me at it until I got it right and understood why.

They were scathing of things that didn't measure up to their standards. Although Wye was small it had several pubs and one of them had an upmarket restaurant. I thought if I got a job there I could be paid to learn about wine and food. My mentors told me that would be a waste of time because the restaurant's owners didn't know anything about sophisticated food or wine.

I worked there for a while. Diners were usually young farmers with fists the size of anvils taking the local shop assistant out to impress her. I could relate to them totally and used to steer them away from the really expensive wines, thinking to myself, 'You should have some of the really cheap plonk because you won't be able to tell the difference between a great wine and some blended rubbish which will go really well with your overdone steak.'

The lessons continued.

'You've got to learn to dance, young Ray. You can't possibly go through life not knowing how to dance. Sooner or later you're going to have to dance with some woman and you'll need to know how.'

I ended up going to dancing class three nights a week because there was a shortage of boys and I could go two nights for free.

It wasn't a total success because I was trying hard to look cool and, although I was short-sighted, I refused to wear my glasses. That was problematic because the boys sat on the bench on one side and had to pick a partner from the bench on the other side of the room. I chose a big bouffant hairstyle and was always two-thirds of the way across the floor heading for a girl before realising she was not so easy on the eye when it was too late to swerve away. I was already committed.

Sometimes it worked in my favour because a good-looking woman would say: 'I liked the way you danced with Shirley, because nobody dances with Shirley and that was very kind of you.'

The professors all talked with the classic Royal Academy of Dramatic Art accent and a strange mixture of exaggeration and understatement which came into play if the results of an experiment were surprising: 'Good Lord! I never thought that would happen in a hundred years.'

Inevitably I picked up something of the RADA voice, being mentored by them. In England it gave you an edge. If that hadn't happened I'm not sure I would have had enough tools to do a lot of what I have done. When you go to the bank manager to get a loan, if you dress and talk the part, then you become convincing.

The accent was knocked out of me in Australia some years later, and today, although most people can tell I was born in England, my class and the locality are harder to pick.

There was time for some more academic education as well. My work was often for theoretical papers they were going to publish and they let me get credit as one of the authors.

For a paper to be inducted into a scientific journal, in those days, it had to be read aloud at a meeting, and there had to be a record of that having happened. We had a lot of these meetings.

One day a professor came to see me.

'Young Ray, you were involved in the paper that Professor Wright has prepared. As part of your ongoing education we would like you to present the paper.'

Although it was written by these guys, I could present it as one of the people involved in it.

I ended up at this meeting, in front of 300 career academics from all over the world. There was no PowerPoint or anything like it. You just stood up and read the paper out loud. It was several pages; you read the abstract summary and then the facts and conclusion. So I did my best RADA delivery and got through it without embarrassing myself. Then my Wye professor friends decided to have some fun.

'Mr Avery,' said one from the floor. 'I noted in the summary that you looked at the different concentrations of plant growth substances and *prima facie* you can actually draw those conclusions, but could there be an artefact from the effect of the osmolarity of these solutions also giving the same outcome?'

I had no bloody idea. It was a test to see how I handled it. All the training I had been given had paid off.

'You're absolutely right,' I said. 'And that's a very interesting question because certainly there are a lot of other paradigms including osmolarity that might have had the same outcome, but to be honest, due to the brevity of time that we have here today it would be imprudent to undertake such a discourse.' The professors smiled back in satisfaction.

While I was at Wye I started studying at the polytechnic and getting some exam qualifications. It was the theory to complement the practice I was doing in my job. The education system was a little dot in the big picture of what I learnt in the real world. Some of the classes were like ancient chemical history compared to the present-day, leading-edge reality I was used to. But I kept studying part-time until I left England. Eventually I got my master's in chemistry and biochemistry.

THE OTHER GREAT THING about all this civilising education I received was that it came just as I was getting very interested in the opposite sex. In fact, my job positively accelerated that interest.

A lot of time was spent in dark rooms, where we were doing work on plant growth substances using wheat seeds. We had fifty-two seeds on a Petri dish, kept in a red-light environment. They grew translucent and when the time was right you cut off sections, threaded them onto thin rods of glass and put them in other Petri dishes. It was all about seeing if you could make them grow better.

It was a long and tedious process, except that when I was

doing it there were young women a couple of years older than me on either side. No man can sit in a dimly lit environment between two beautiful women for eight hours a day without some physiological response.

I ended up having a liaison with an eighteen-year-old lab technician who was also a virgin. The red light cast a glow on one side of her face and one side of my face and it led to an awful lot of fun. In fact, it led to us making love all over Wye College. The glasshouses were a good location because they were full of almost tropical growth and you weren't disturbed. Unless you picked the wrong one, and the irrigation system turned on while you were there and you got completely soaked. Which made it a bit obvious what had been going on when you came running out.

I didn't encounter the Woman in the White Dress but I was learning how to conduct the search.

I always told the girls I got involved with that I was never going to get married or have children. And I wasn't, back then.

Mainly, I was emerging as a proper human being and trying to find some sort of comfort with another person and a gentler way of living.

As well as those stirrings, my entrepreneurial instincts were also coming into play. Having a motorbike brought even more freedom. In particular, it was easy to get to Canterbury, which was the nearest big town. I got a job managing a petrol station there.

Part of my job was to drive a Commer van around on the weekend in the middle of winter, delivering kerosene from a mini-tanker inside the van to people who had kerosene heaters in their little cottages. That was a sideline that came with the petrol station business. It took from about 5.30 until 9.30 at night, going around all the villages in the snow.

We kept trialling people and they didn't like it because it was truly terrible driving around in the snow freezing your nuts off. So I ended up doing it. You could get a little kerosene heater for cars to stop your engine oil freezing, and I put that in the passenger side of the van, which was probably highly dangerous.

I realised a lot of the little old ladies on the run were housebound and needed other things, like matches, candles, cigarettes and crisps for the evening. We had a shop in the garage so every morning I loaded up the van with stock from there and had a mini-mart in the back of the Commer. That was a marginal failure to begin with because the fumes from the heater infiltrated everything and people complained their cigarettes smelt of kerosene. I fixed that by getting a bigger tank on a trailer behind the van.

The petrol station had a mechanics' workshop attached. I used to go down to watch them at work and learn a bit about mechanical repairs. When the mechanics wanted to set up in their own right I suggested getting a lease on a petrol station. I offered to put up some money and go in on the deal with them.

So we did. Then we started buying and selling used cars. We were always strapped for cash.

There was no electronic banking in those days; it was just cheques and taking cash to the bank to deposit it. I had soon bought a lease on a second petrol station, at Ramsgate. To get around the cash-flow problems, I took, say, a thousand pounds from my account at a bank in Ramsgate. Then I went back to Canterbury, where my main bank was, and deposited the money into the account before the withdrawal had time to show up. That meant for the two days it took to process the transactions I had two thousand pounds for my one thousand. That was enough money to keep going and we waited anxiously for a car to sell so we could pay back the money we didn't have. We took risks and finally got some serious money together.

It probably wasn't what my mentors had in mind for me. But I had changed a huge amount in my time at Wye. There are two photos taken not that long apart. One was when I arrived, and I am sitting in the front in my old grey jacket but with some suede shoes I managed to find, and I'm just a little boy who is very pleased to be sitting on the grass with the girls. A year or so later and another photo, and I'm standing at the back with the men, looking even more pleased, in my flash new Italian suit. The professors have worked their magic on me.

Part of me wanted to stay at Wye forever but all these other things were working away at my mind. My thesis is that you eat up jobs in three years and then you just start repeating yourself.

I'm very thankful they showed me another world. Ironically, it turned out to be a world I couldn't enjoy. Once I was moving in circles they trained me to move in, although I enjoyed it, it was made very clear that I did not belong there.

FIVE

E-Type personality

I went to work in 1965 at South-Eastern Laboratories, a privately owned analytical testing facility in Canterbury which contracted to local government authorities to do official testing of water and sewage quality, and food and drug analysis. It also catered for ordinary people who wanted things analysed — someone who wanted a second opinion on the sample that had been used to convict them of drink-driving, for instance. I stayed about four years and ended up as senior analyst.

The job suited me because it paid more than being a technician at Wye, and I could continue to run my other enterprises around it. I also needed somewhere nearer the polytechnic, because I was taking papers in chemistry and biochemistry.

At South-Eastern, I was subject to another knowledge explosion as my appetite for applied science was fed every day. I arrived with basic chemical knowledge but it was mainly about plants. Now I learnt about paint, chemistry, making anything and analysing everything. There was nothing on this planet whose contents I couldn't work out as a consequence of what I learned there.

The professional scientists there were not as elegant as the team at Wye, but with an average age of about fifty-five they had years and years of knowledge, and I loved absorbing all that. They had their eccentricities, but they were scientists' eccentricities. One old chemist, a Mr Woods, had a ritual every morning when he arrived at work. He took off his shoe, which had a circular heel, and used a small screwdriver on his penknife to turn the heel around so that the wear was even. Apparently, this meant his shoes lasted for years.

There was nothing eccentric about his professional abilities, for which I was often grateful. One of my jobs was to analyse the water for the borough of Camden. This arrived in big carboys and I had to measure how much was in them, which I did by siphoning it into measuring cylinders.

That took time, so I got on with other jobs while the carboys emptied. Inevitably, I got engrossed once and forgot my emptying carboy so the cylinder overflowed.

'What shall I do?' I asked Mr Woods, staring at the spreading puddle on the floor.

'Well, there's thirteen and a half tiles covered,' he said, and put a ruler into the pool, 'and it's two millimetres deep,' and then he worked out the total area and thus the volume of liquid I had let spill.

I was always being impressed by what these guys could work out. We got in samples of honey that we had to check to see if it came from France as claimed. You put it under a microscope, looked at the pollen grains, then went to a reference book which illustrated every pollen grain from every country in the world — because they are all different shapes and sizes and colours. They are beautiful things — some look like hand grenades and some have furry bits on them, but they are all different. So you could say with certainty whether honey was from France or had never been anywhere near it. Often, the more experienced scientists didn't need the book. They just looked at the honey and said, 'That's from Somerset.'

The customers were something else again, and I was often the first person to meet them and find out what they wanted. It tends to be a certain sort of person who needs to have something analysed by a professional laboratory.

One day a man in his seventies, wearing a raincoat, presented himself.

'My wife is trying to kill me,' he announced, producing a jar of cocoa from under his raincoat and placing it on the table in front of me.

'Oh, I don't think so,' I said, but I knew enough about people and psychology by now to at least appear to take him seriously. 'Why do you think that?'

'Well, every time I go to bed or get ready for bed, I have my cocoa, and then I'm on the toilet all night, shitting constantly.'

I thought he probably had irritable bowel syndrome, but didn't say so.

'Hold on a sec,' I said, 'and I'll go into the lab and confer with one of my colleagues.'

I really had no idea what to do but I went into the lab. I couldn't stop laughing once I got there but somehow I managed to explain to Mr Woods what the story was. He took some of the cocoa and put it on a slide under a microscope.

'Look at that,' he said.

'What?' I said, peering into the microscope.

'The cocoa is made by a freeze-dried process which produces the nicely rounded granules you can see. But there are also some angular granules visible, which don't belong to cocoa.'

He put a sample in a test tube with a little alkali.

'There you go,' he concluded. 'Phenyphaline.'

'What's that?'

'It's an acid base indicator, but it's also the main ingredient in laxative chocolate.'

So I went back out and said, 'It looks as though there may be something going on.'

The old man ended up taking his wife to court and we gave evidence. She admitted everything.

'Why did you do it?' asked the judge.

'I wanted to curb his unwanted sexual advances,' she confessed.

Giving evidence in court wasn't always so straightforward, although every customer provided an opportunity to learn something new. There seemed to be a procession of sausage makers advertising their wares as 'Mrs Smith's Natural Sausages, Preservative-Free' and being taken to court for having bangers that were full of preservatives. There was a simple test we did to check this.

Once I went to court and read my statement in a sausage case.

'I am Ray Avery, scientist, and I have analysed these sausages and found them to contain 220 parts sulphur dioxide and this would seem to breach the regulations . . .'

The butcher had a lawyer, and it was odd for them to be defending the thing because usually they just paid the fine.

'I noted, Mr Avery,' said the lawyer, 'that there's another

signature above yours on this document. It says "senior technician Margaret Wilson". What did she actually do?'

'She did the bench work and I checked the results,' I explained.

'But you've told us, Mr Avery, that you analysed these sausages. I put it to you, sir, that you're a liar.'

And the case was thrown out. This prompted me to take a healthy interest in the preparation of legal documentation.

Apart from people being poisoned themselves, there was a huge number who believed their neighbours were trying to do away with their cat and were only too happy to collect turds for us to check for traces of poison.

Worse ingredients were involved in the case of a woman who had gone on a diet which consisted of bread and a special powder. She wasn't happy and had complained to the Department of Health, who sent us the powder to investigate.

The SOP for cases like this was to give a rat the equivalent of a meal of whatever we were analysing, so we fed this powder to some rats. It turned out to be a gum that swelled inside to make you feel full, and when we went back to check, the rats were dead. They had all blown up to look like balloons with a little foot in each corner.

Other people came to see us because they wanted us to help them make money. These were the ones least likely to act on what we discovered if it wasn't what they wanted to hear.

One man had found some fluid to use for cleaning and lubricating watches which was much cheaper than anything else around. We checked it for him and at first glance it seemed fine, but there was a proviso.

'If you use it,' I told him, 'you need to not sell it to people but do some stability tests on it. You need to put it into some watches and let them run for at least six months to make sure nothing is going to happen. If the oil goes rancid or decays, it might do something to the workings. I don't know what, you've got to check it. It's got all the same physical characteristics in terms of its viscosity and temperature stability but we just don't know.'

So he cleaned some watches with it, decided he could start selling it, and in about six months all the watches he had handled were brought back because they had seized up and stopped.

More enjoyable was the alcohol testing. All bonded spirits, such as whisky and rum, brought into England were subject to excise tax, and their alcohol was tested to determine the amount of duty, a practice dating back hundreds of years. We took samples. To make sure they were representative, if it was a big shipment, we sometimes ended up with fifty little bottles, or whole barrels were sent to us.

We had to take them back to the lab and distil them to extract the alcohol to measure it. We finished up with almost neat alcohol in one place and everything else from the spirit in another. And we put them into big containers and stored them for our annual party at the end of the year. Then we blended them back into something that we thought was the best possible brandy or whisky. We did that over a Christmas meal and we got absolutely trolleyed while we were eating meat samples that were also being tested for analysis.

We always had a brilliant lunch because it was comprised of all the food samples that had been brought in by the Ministry of Health.

'What will we have for lunch today? I'll try a little of this ham and a little of that ham.' And if the ham was particularly good, we might have to request another sample, just to make sure.

The other aspect of testing that involved alcohol was the high number of people trying to beat drink-driving convictions. I tried to be humane and find out whether it was even worth doing because it was going to cost someone a lot of money.

'How did they pick you up?' I asked one young petrol-head.

'You know that big straight bit of road, on the way to Ashford? Well I took out three lampposts.' I told him not to waste his money.

The ones I got most tired of were the seminal stain guys. When you went out to reception you were confronted with a man carrying a brown paper bag. He inevitably opened it and produced some ominously stained women's underwear.

'I reckon my wife's getting it on with the milkman, and I want you to check it for seminal stains.'

They were coming for two reasons: to get the analysis done firstly, but also for some sort of psychotherapy. Often, if they didn't get the result they were after, they wanted us to come up with other ways to find out if they were being cheated on.

Eventually, if it was just about anybody with a brown paper bag, I pretended not to be the person they needed to see. 'I'll just get a scientist who's qualified to help you,' I said and ran to find someone else to hand them on to. I had done my time on psycho patrol.

Through it all though, especially when we were looking at more serious things, like claims of chemical discharges from factories into the water, I was taught to do everything to the highest standard. I learnt that if you went to court, your evidence had to be impeccable and that a mistake could cost people their livelihoods and, in some cases, their lives. I was becoming an ethical scientist. So later, when I was producing drugs or building plants to make them in, I understood the importance of best practice. It was a scientific indoctrination where quality pervaded every activity.

Now, when I see some of the crimes being committed in the developing world, I don't understand it. If you're used to having quality scientific ethics, it's inconceivable that you would give bad stuff to people in the name of aid. It's hard to understand, but not hard to believe — we often tested kids' toys and found they contained huge amounts of heavy metals in the paint.

And, of course, this was the perfect place to develop my ability to work out quality Standard Operating Procedures for any activity. Sometimes I found myself visualising an SOP for everyday activities, like opening a door: 'Go to the door, stand with your feet apart, balance, reach forward, grab hold of the handle, turn it anti-clockwise until it meets the finished excursion, pull the door towards you whilst . . .' That was very important for training people in the developing world later on.

At the lab I learnt another SOP that I have often applied to problems in other areas of life. Someone came in with a product containing twenty-two ingredients that might have involved sixty chemical entities. To unravel and analyse something like that is a long and difficult process.

'The problem is,' I said to them, 'we have this huge elephant we need to eat. It's obviously too big, so what can we do? Let's start with the toenail. Could you eat that?' And each day you ate a little bit more and a little bit more until finally you had eaten the whole elephant. You just had to break it down into bite-sized bits.

One of my friends at the lab had a father who was a bookie and he was as practical as they come because he had to work out the odds on the spot. You could throw any sum at him.

'Take six times twenty-three times minus seventeen minus thirty-five plus one hundred and thirty-six, what's the answer?'

'Oh, 1322.555.'

When we asked him how he did it he said he just broke it into little bites of information, and calculated one at a time. But he could never remember where he parked his car.

We applied the elephant-eating SOP to lots of things, but other projects didn't need that much finesse. 'Electronic testing' of condoms, for instance, didn't mean an electronic current was sent through the condom on the off chance Superman might end up buying it. It just meant we electronically filled the rubbers with a known pressure of water to see if they leaked.

That was great fun for us technicians because, if you throw a condom full of water at somebody and they put their hand up to deflect it, it comes round like something in a cartoon and whacks them on the head. And when you drop a water-filled condom from three storeys, it forms a beautiful tear shape, then, when it hits the ground it splashes anyone nearby but also disappears, so they don't know what's happened.

The other thing we occasionally dropped out of windows was teddy bears. We had to test them for flammability by holding them out the window and setting fire to them with a lighter. Once one flared up and burnt my hand. I dropped it and it fell into a rubbish bin full of oily rags which burst into flame.

Applied science took many forms. After a friend of mine got an ingrown toenail and went to the doctor he came back with his whole foot in a cast. About the same time I got an ingrown toenail too.

'I'm not going to a doctor. I can fix it,' I told myself. After all, in the lab I had access to local anaesthetics, but the stuff we had was the version for horses, and it didn't say anywhere on it how strong it was. I put some in a needle, stuck it in my foot to numb it and chopped the nail off.

But when I tried to get up to walk, I couldn't because my

whole leg had gone to sleep. I couldn't feel a thing for about eight hours.

Along with the learning went some teaching. Once a technician came to me and he was holding a small flask that I could see was beginning to boil. I held it up to my eyes to have a look at it.

'What have you got in here?' I asked.

'It's alcohol concentrate with nitric acid.'

'Shit!'

Just as I placed the flask in the sink it exploded. My lab coat melted, and if it had blown up a second or two earlier we would both have been killed or blinded at best. In the days before safety guidelines and masks and such, many organic chemists had fingers blown off.

Our experience was practical across all sorts of areas. We analysed pollen not just to tell where the honey was from but sometimes to tell where a murder suspect had been by working out the source of the pollen attached to his clothing. That knowledge, and that way of acquiring knowledge, becomes invaluable when you're designing things.

I was also making the most of life away from work, which was why it was important we did a comparative titration exercise every morning. Titration involved controlling the drips from a small valve and stopping them exactly when you needed to, so you didn't go over a certain limit. Hand-eye co-ordination was crucial to our work in lots of ways, so we all had to be tested every morning to see how good our control was.

It was another example of quality scientific ethics. Everything we did might end up in court, so quality was paramount.

'Mr Avery's titration standard deviation is not acceptable today.' And the reason it varied was that I might have been on the town or not had enough sleep the night before.

Above: Working on the Avery grin in one of my grey-on-grey uniforms in 1953. Despite what life had been like at home I could still manage a smile for the camera.

Below left: In 1961 England was about to come out of its post-war malaise – my recovery would take a little longer, despite the fashionable 'do.
Right: In 1964 I had managed to find some cheekbones but lost the smile. These were the years of the young man about town.

Above and *below*: On my way to finding the Woman in the White Dress, I found several others who were happy to act as sports car accessories. These shots are taken between 1965 and 1970, years during which I grew into a successful young man whom I came to dislike.

Above: Wye College was a major turning point, although in this picture, taken in 1962, I don't fully belong. Instead, still insecure and uncomfortable, I sat myself (bottom row, far left) with the 'girls'.

Below: Two years later and I have been fully integrated into professorial attitudes and elegant modes of behaviour by my mentors. That's me second from left in the back row, one of the boys.

Above: The white coats are the only professional thing in this 1988 photo of the Douglas Pharmaceuticals team. Great colleagues and workers, appalling photographic subjects.

Below: A highlight of 1994's return visit to the UK was meeting up with Jack Wise, humanitarian teacher and a man who almost certainly saved my life.

Above: Working on construction of the intraocular lens laboratory in Eritrea in 1993 – I'm just making it look easy for the photographer.

Below: At the Tilganga Eye Centre in Kathmandu, Nepal, 1988 – use of the word 'home' was accurate as this was another family I had made for myself with my work.

Above: After twenty years of war between Eritrea and Ethiopia, signs of Massawa's status as the Italy of Africa could still be seen in what was left of its buildings in 2003.

Below: With a cataract patient in Nepal in 2003 – the work we did there proved to me that it really was possible to eat an elephant if you used the correct SOP.

Above: The Medicine Mondiale Liferaft incubator will save thousands, if not millions, of lives and is a fraction of the cost charged for current models.

Below: For just $10, a lens like this can return sight to cataract sufferers in the developing world. Plus, like the Liferaft, it's a very sexy piece of industrial design.

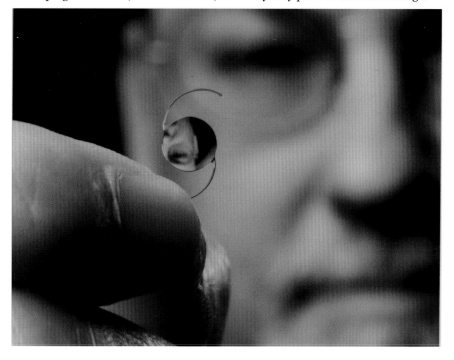

Above: Finally, the Woman in White found me – my stunning bride Anna Kiousis and myself on our wedding day in Sydney, 2007.

Below: Myself with the most adorable Anglo-Kiwi-Australian-Greek child ever born, my daughter Miss Amelia Avery.

WITH THE INCOME FROM my job and other interests, I was becoming quite the man about town. I pulled up outside our building, parked my shiny MG in the carpark and marched in wearing my dark suit, dark trench coat, black leather gloves and patent shoes. Not a trace of the grey uniform and brown shoes, and with a well-practised RADA accent I was just the right sort of person to send to meet clients.

When I started to make some money, I spent it: the fast car, the Italian suit and restaurants. The little orphan boy had made it and liked having the waiters treat him like he was special. I was inside Claridge's looking out.

Later I got invited to hunt balls and poetry readings and to stay overnight at country estates. But what I thought was flash wasn't really flash because I was just buying it. I wasn't entitled to it, born to it, like the people I was mixing with. They knew it, but I didn't. In London terms, I was a bit too Oxford Street rather than Park Lane.

The men I met and circulated with all had their shoes handmade by somebody and their jackets made by somebody else. When I found this out I whipped down to Park Lane and handed over money for the same. A shoemaker measured my foot and got a pen knife and started hacking at a bit of wood to make a last for my shoe. Somewhere there's still a bloke with a mould for shoes in the shape of my feet. Handmade shoes were probably about $800 in today's money, and I thought that was great.

I got a cravat and had a hunting jacket made, so I could fit in when I went to the hunt balls. It was all about fitting in. For the young girls around town I was flash, but the only people I impressed were people who were easily impressed.

Cars were a major passion and a natural progression: from pumping gas in the petrol station, to hanging out in the workshop and repairing cars to modifying them for racing.

I fell in love for the first time when I was twelve and saw the first Sunbeam Alpine white sports car at a local Rootes dealership. It was the best, sexiest thing I'd ever seen in my life. Even now I love driving fast. It's to do with being absorbed in the moment. I love the man-and-car-together feeling and changing gears perfectly or going to a form of light speed.

When I had the petrol stations I used to go racing on weekends and used the garages to speed up the cars. It was hopeless really, because my only strategy for making cars go faster was to put a bigger engine in and go through an array of carburettors and try to get as much gas going into it as possible.

Cars were also part of the SOP for girls. Who could resist an MGA or E-Type Jag? When I took a girl out, I made sure there was champagne and flowers and chocolate in the boot.

Most of the girls I got together with were from the poly where I was studying. The roll was about 2000 and they far outnumbered the boys. There was one girl I knew vaguely from there who was good-looking and, for the times, really out there — almost punky. She used to hitch down to the coast to go to discos at Margate and Ramsgate in the Mods and Rockers days. Often before she left she popped into the petrol station for some bits and pieces.

One weekend I was going to Ramsgate and offered her a lift. We had a fling for a while. Afterwards she came in when she knew I was going down and that was her ride. Eventually I worked out she was being used one way and another by all sorts of people and I thought she deserved better than that. I tried to make her see she didn't need to go to these discos and let herself be exploited. I offered her a job behind the counter at the petrol station.

But she wasn't interested and it taught me that you can't change some people.

Given there was no way I wanted to get married or settle down, my attitude to the girls I got together with was the same as it was to everyone else: I thought everybody should be better off for having met me. I loved women and I loved being around women, because they were gentle and safe compared with all the other things that had happened to me and especially compared to the main woman in my life up to then — my mother.

But there were two things that caused systematic failure in the relationships.

One was my feeling that my girlfriends needed to understand the world wasn't beautiful. I went out with one who worked in a bank and lived at home with her mum and dad. She had never experienced anything bad in her life. I went out with her for about six months and she was close to the Woman in the White Dress but she didn't really have any understanding of the world at large. She didn't, from my perspective, understand that it was a *Once Were Warriors* society that we lived in. I got frustrated and felt alone when people didn't understand that, and it was often a precursor to things not working out.

At the same time, I always felt bereft if I got into any kind of argument with them. Having been brought up around all that violence, one might imagine I had some violent tendencies, but that background had the opposite effect on me. I abhorred violence and if there were conflicts, my SOP was to do a runner, because I didn't want to be around it. I wanted a beautiful life. I wanted everybody to be happy and to love each other.

The other issue with women was mistrust, because with my mother I had done all those things to make her love me, like making cups of tea and walking halfway to the hospital to walk home with her, and that sometimes was met with good outcomes and sometimes with bad outcomes, depending on what had happened in her day. I had developed the belief that women were unpredictable and that worried me greatly.

But I kept looking and not necessarily in the right place. I had an entire SOP around discos, which became part of my daily routine. By the time I had done the kerosene run, which I kept doing long after I needed to, it was nine o'clock, which was also when the garage shut. So then I did the books — totting up the petrol we had sold and what was bought over the counter. That took me through to 11. There were no restaurants open at that hour, so I had a choice of going home to cook something or, Wednesday to Saturday, going to the disco.

There was a man there who did food for the stupefied and insane — spaghetti Bolognese toasted sandwiches and spaghetti Bolognese upside-down pizza and not much else. But I had been freezing my nuts off driving around country lanes late at night and getting in and out of the van and working up an appetite at the garage, so that was what I ate.

Now, what all this meant, and which inadvertently worked in my favour, was that all the other blokes at the disco had already been there for a few hours getting legless. I turned up in my sports car, dressed as flash as I could be and, because I was starving, ignored everyone and headed for the food. So I acquired this aloof, unattainable mystique. Instead of me having to ask a girl to dance, they made the first move. And once I was warm and the carbohydrates kicked in, I was certainly ready to play up.

I was getting good at reading signals, too. The social anthropology skills, from all those years in orphanages watching people, came into play. The key thing was to observe how a girl danced. If you mastered dancing like her, your chances of success were monumental.

The result was usually a one-night stand and that was what I had set my place up for. I had the light switch with the dimmer and tape recorder with the right music and a bar — the whole shabby thing.

After a couple of years that wears thin though, and there is not even the possibility of being involved with another human being in any real sense. The girls were pretty, but they were Barbie dolls with bouffant hairstyles — nothing like the Woman in the White Dress. I had a very clear image of her, and I couldn't see her anywhere. Although these girls were very easy on the eye, they weren't particularly bright, and I needed to be able to talk about Descartes or the meaning of life.

They weren't impressed by that. They were impressed if I was in a shop and produced a credit card to pay for something.

'Are you a rep?' one gasped once, because in those days only someone like a sales rep had anything as flash as a credit card. And as far as stimulating conversation went, it was no better when I aimed higher on the social ladder and went to hunt balls with the 'Who-are-you-where-are-you-from-what-do-you-do?' crowd.

In fact, towards the end I tried to avoid the disco altogether. Instead I drove an extra twenty-five kilometres up the motorway to a café for a feed.

Sometimes things started out well with a girl but ended up as pure farce. Most days that I went to poly we had a one-hour lunch break. The poly was only a few hundred metres from my flat and I could usually find a willing girl to come home with me in the break. Lunch in those cases often lasted till the middle of the afternoon.

On one occasion, another girl I had been seeing in Ramsgate had decided to come up on the bus and surprise me. I was in bed with this other woman, which would not have been a problem if my mate had not come into the flat to drop something off and left the door on the latch so it wasn't locked.

Suddenly Margaret from Ramsgate appeared in the doorway. What could I say?

'Hello, Margaret. This is Jane.'

Margaret whacked me with her handbag and stormed off downstairs. All I could hear was the breaking of glass as she worked her way around my car. Thankfully she only did the lights. Just one headlight was about $350 at today's rate. And she could've gone round the panels as well.

Another girl I saw about this time was a brewery magnate's daughter who invited me to their home one weekend. I knew I was in trouble the moment I arrived at the start of their driveway, because I couldn't see the house from there.

I knocked on the huge oak door and nobody answered. I walked around the back and there they were having afternoon tea on the lawn. I couldn't actually see a butler but I kept expecting one to appear.

I had a nice jacket on and the whole deal. I had brought the E-Type Jag so they'd think I was flash, but that was a mistake. It was just one of the subtleties that the professors at Wye had not been able to teach me.

The father refused to allow his daughter to go out to the theatre in the sports car because he thought it was too dangerous, so he told me to take one of their cars that was out in the garage. They had a DS Citroën, the kind with the hydraulic suspension.

'You'll need to take it down to the garage to get it filled up first,' he said, 'and have a good time at the theatre.'

I pulled up at the pump, next to one of those big concrete bollards that petrol stations used to have. I swung the door open and switched the motor off, and the bloody car went down on its hydraulics and the door got stuck on the bollard.

I couldn't get the door to close so we drove all the way home hanging onto the door. Things got worse when we arrived.

'Put the car in the barn and we'll go in and have a nightcap,' said the girl. So I went into the barn and she came too, and in the darkness away from Daddy it all started to happen. But she had contact lenses and while we were pashing one dropped out. It could have been anywhere on her. She started to take bits of clothing off to try to find it.

At that point the whole place was illuminated and there was Daddy gazing at the spectacle of a wrecked car and his daughter in a state of undress and that was the end of the date.

ALL THIS WHILE THE money kept coming in. I had too many things on the go at once. I loved money. I kept doing the kerosene run long after I needed to. I hated letting one revenue stream go even when I had acquired so many others.

I met a sausage manufacturer at a trade function who said, 'I want you to analyse all my sausages for protein and preservative.' He was always getting busted for putting too much preservative in his sausages. It was a big contract and I could see an opportunity for me. I made the most of my social skills.

'I'll do the contract for you,' I said. 'You just deliver the samples to me and I'll sort it out.' I took the samples to another analytical testing laboratory as a client and then just acted as a middle man. Before long, I realised I could do the whole thing. I bought an interest in the second laboratory that I was working with and eventually bought them out over two to three years, setting up my own lab.

So my daily SOP was that I went to one lab, did everything, then ducked across town at lunchtime to the other lab.

I loved getting my pay packet from the lab and just shoving it into a drawer without taking the money out. I used to open the drawer and look at all the unopened pay packets and congratulate myself on having made it. I bought an apartment on a prestigious street, renovated it and developed it into two — I was a mini-property-developer along with everything else.

The double job gig eventually became too much so I left the analytical test lab and took another job at Shell Research that one of my old Wye professors had recommended to me. It was in Sittingbourne, a small, quiet provincial town, and that appealed because everything else was getting so complicated — especially with the two labs — and I reasoned that if money wasn't making me happy, perhaps moving to a sleepy little place would bring back some of the old Wye magic with its gentle lifestyle.

The set-up was in an old ex-army barracks that had been converted into a research centre. We did research on herbicides, fungicides and weedkillers.

But I couldn't help myself. I hired out some sheds and set up a garage where Shell workers could drop off their cars in the morning and have them serviced before they went home.

I was working on one particular thing, which was the role of metalloproteins on the Hill reaction of photosynthesis. We wrote several papers on that and I was one of the world experts from a pool of around fifteen people globally. I was quite excited by that and kept waiting for people to bring it up at parties, but it never happened.

So I was still no happier and the romantic side of things was getting out of hand.

I had a girlfriend in Margate, one in Canterbury, one in Ashford and one in Wye. The guys thought I was a legend because every time we had a function I brought a different girl from a different area.

But one day I was riding my motorbike on the motorway, after some idiot had crashed into the roundabout and taken it out. In the middle of the night they put up a temporary roundabout using fourty-four-gallon drums with lights on. Somebody stole the lights from one side. I came around a corner, saw only the lights on the other side, realised too late what was happening and smacked into the drums.

I came off the bike, rolled over once to break my collarbone and a few more times to break bones in my leg at each turn. I was left unable to move in a spreading sea of petrol.

A guy turned up in one of those three-wheeled Bond fibreglass cars. He stopped to help and came over, with a glowing fag hanging out the corner of his mouth.

'Are you okay?' he said.

'I bloody will be if you don't blow me up. Get away,' I yelled back.

He got me off to the hospital and I was there for about two weeks of nightmare. I could hardly do a thing. When I went to the toilet and got up to wipe myself, you could guarantee I would fall over and get jammed in the stall where I'd have to wait up to an hour before someone found me.

During that time all the women I had been seeing wanted to find out what had happened to me. Some of them came miles on a bus, some weren't far away, but they all turned up on the same day — Margate, Canterbury, Ashford and Wye. I looked out the window and there was a flock of them. I was just too sick and too worried to deal with it.

Worlds collided — all these private worlds that I had managed to keep apart. They were quite upset. Although I didn't want to deal with it, I was also just mortified that they were so upset because I genuinely cared about them. I tried to be nice to all of them and I thought I had been. But I hadn't been a good person.

And when they went off and told me how they felt — well, it was that contradiction I had never got over with my mother. One moment things were fine and peaceful, the next all hell was breaking loose.

It was winter when I was finally allowed out of hospital. I went back to my luxury apartment which looked over a bit of a park, and everything looked dark and dreary. The miners were on strike, so there was no electricity. I was still hobbling around and I went down to the pub to try to get a pie or something to eat, and they were out of pies. There had been a rush on food. There was nobody in the shops and I ended up cooking residues of whatever was in cans in the cupboard. I thought: 'There has got to be a better place to live than this, this is just terrible.'

There were several niggling occurrences that made me think I was living in the wrong country. I kept my laminated driver's licence in my back pocket which meant that over time it developed a curve from having my bum pressing on it. To have it renewed you took it to an office and put it into a little tray on the other side of which stood a man with a peaked cap. On this occasion, he swivelled the tray around and picked up the licence, looked at it disdainfully, rocked back and forth on the balls of his feet, and bent it on the edge of the desk, trying and failing to straighten it. Then he cut it up with a pair of scissors and gave me a new one, saying: 'Try and find a better way of keeping that, sir.'

When you took a train you got a ticket with two halves, outward bound and inward bound, separated by a line across the middle. When you went through the checkpoint going into the station, an attendant clicked it in each direction. If you handed it over the wrong way around they wouldn't touch it. They stood back, holding their hands in the air to avoid any risk of coming into contact with the offending item. 'Please present your ticket in the right way, sir.' They wouldn't turn it around and click it for you. That wasn't playing by the rules.

And when I was doing renovations on my apartment, the building inspectors came around — always two of them — with their tape measures and I was told my hot-water cylinder couldn't go in the space I wanted because it was two inches off the right size. It was exactly the kind of regimentation I hated and it seemed to be getting worse and worse.

I'd had enough. It was time for a change. I could do with a fresh start. I had no idea where I was going but I decided to sell up.

I didn't belong anywhere. I'd developed an accent to get accepted by upper-middle-class society, and I was a great raconteur in their social circles, but I never belonged there. I didn't ever feel comfortable there. I also didn't feel comfortable at the other end of society, meeting people who knew me from the council houses.

THINGS WERE BECOMING unravelled in my head. I wasn't happy with who I was. I wasn't in love. Running petrol stations was pretty ordinary. The laboratories were functioning fine but I was only needed when there was a problem with a client.

There was no place for me to go because I'd achieved everything that I thought would make me happy. I had money, acquaintances — people who owned castles and nightclubs and stuff like that — and I could pretty much get any woman I wanted, but I wasn't happy and I thought there had to be somewhere else.

I decided to go and see what the rest of the world was like. I didn't know anything about it. My life had been spent in southern England or London. I'd never read much about the world at large. Geography had not been one of my main research interests in library days. Most of my reading had been inquiries into how things worked and romantic stories like *Treasure Island* and the myths of the Greek gods.

The only overseas trips I had made were to Majorca for dirty weekends and to France for breakfast. I had a friend who owned a travel agency who would give me a free fare if I could arrange four girls to go on one of his packages.

Spain was hot and I would be able to relax and think about what I wanted to do next. I didn't have to worry about money. I sold all my interests to my partners and other people and I was just going to go down to the ferry.

I knew I wasn't coming back. I was turning my back on the dark hole of England. I think there was probably also the thought that everything bad that had ever happened to me was to do with that country.

I had a vague idea I might end up in Australia because a friend of a friend's father had visited there for eight months and decided to return to England, and his primary reason for coming back was that he couldn't get any decent bread.

I didn't know it, but I was on my way home for the first time. Home was a place I had never seen, on the other side of the world, as far from England and the man I had become as it was possible to get.

SIX

The making of a New Zealander

I planned to hitch and see where the road led me. It was 1973, I was twenty-five, cashed up and had no ties. After a couple of days on the road I ended up in a little town near Munich, where I found a bed in a *pension*.

The next morning I saw a bus parked on the other side of the road. The passengers were about thirty Australians and New Zealanders who were taking it from London to Kathmandu. They had set up their tents and camped in a field nearby after having a big flare-up in Munich the night before. The morning was well advanced by the time I went over to say hello.

'What are you guys doing still here?' I asked.

'We just went to this beer fest thing,' one said, 'and the driver's run off with the wife of one of the passengers. So we're stuck.'

'Is he coming back?'

'We don't know.'

They had one other driver, a man called Fred who was one of the tour organisers. Fred was really just a passenger who had been on the bus from Kathmandu to London and now wanted to do the return trip. That was his only experience of being a tour leader.

'You can't drive a bus, can you?' said Fred.

'I've got a heavy goods vehicle licence,' I told him. 'I'm not qualified to drive in the UK, but I can drive in Europe.'

He wasn't interested in my explanations.

'But can you drive the bus?'

'Yeah. I can drive it.'

'If we give you £20 a week, can you drive it to Kathmandu?'

I wasn't keen and while we were discussing it the original driver — and the woman he had shot through with — reappeared. She went off to sort things out with her husband, and I was off the hook as far as the driving went.

'We'll give you a lift if you like,' said Fred, so I became a paying passenger, although I got a discount because the bus broke down constantly and I helped fix it. The trip was supposed to take three months but ended up being more like eight.

For me it was good because I could see all those countries but still have some structure to my journey. This was my first exposure to different cultures and countries and, of course, to the sort of poverty you see in places like India, Pakistan and Afghanistan.

We crossed the Indian-Pakistan border about six times and it was always exciting. There were arms dealers at both ends of the Khyber Pass. You could buy just about anything. Lots of the Australian guys bought handguns. I don't know what they were planning to do with them. One kept posting bits of his gun back to his granny over about four months.

We were like a strange-moving 1960s beast going through these countries, and my social anthropology side got a good workout in yet another new environment. For one thing, with my knowledge of pharmacology, I was the closest thing the bus had to a doctor.

For another thing, it was the seventies and the active romantic life on board meant there was plenty that would have kept a real doctor busy.

The worst case involved one particular girl. Many of the places we went through were small villages which had very conservative views about women. When they saw the girls wearing shorts and t-shirts with no bras, the men in these villages took them for hookers and treated them like it too.

Once, in a village that specialised in beautiful woven rugs, a local was yelling at one of the girls: 'One metre of carpet for a half hour of sex!' She disappeared and when she turned up again she looked like she had earned enough rugs to carpet an airport terminal.

This girl took me aside later.

'Ray,' she said, 'I've got a bit of a sore wozzer, do you want to have a look?'

'Not particularly,' I said, but she made me have a look at it.

'I'm not sure what it is, but I don't like it,' I said. 'It looks like you've got syphilis from what I've read.'

So we went off to the hospital and sure enough she had. The treatment in those days was 50ccs of penicillin in each bum cheek. That's a fair lump and it's a deep intramuscular injection — it forces its way into the tissue, a bit like having a tennis ball injected in each buttock, and you can't walk properly for quite a while after you get it.

'You need to tell everyone who you bonked on the bus,' I said, 'because they're going to be infected and will need to get shots.'

So shortly after that, there was a procession of guys all walking like they had just absorbed a tennis ball.

It was amazing watching girls who had got on the bus in London with their painted nails and bouffant hairstyles being transformed into wispy creatures wearing saris and with studs in their noses and navels. They didn't completely assimilate. At the evening meal they usually had fried spam and eggs instead of trying all the glorious food that was available in the places we visited.

One couple got married at a temple in Isfahan in Iran. We all got dressed up to go. Some of us had suits made by the local tailor. Mine was a beautiful white outfit and the girl I had struck up a relationship with had a white dress on as well.

That was when I learnt something about the developing world that is as true today as it was then — there is shit everywhere. We were all set to go to the wedding when a horse standing near us lifted its tail and sprayed crap all over us.

There was nothing we could do. When we arrived at the temple everybody turned around to see where the smell was coming from and we had to stay at the back.

Because the bus was its own society and not part of a larger one, strange things happened. Two of the girls decided to have a relationship with me — a classic ménage à trois. They were the ones who worked it through. They went off holding hands together one day, decided what was going to happen and came back and told me.

The three of us used to go to bed together at night, and in the morning people brought us breakfast. Even we found it bizarre that they did that without blinking an eyelid.

That relationship carried on for about six months. One of the girls was Australian and that meant I was going to go to Australia to have a look around. The other girl had friends in New Zealand and she took off there.

WHEN I GOT ON THE plane to go to Darwin from Kathmandu I was wearing cotton clothes with little embroidered buttons and generally looked like the biggest hippie on the planet. As a result, when I got off the plane in Darwin they were poking wires down my rucksacks to see if there were drugs in there.

I started out in the north and the worlds collided because I still had the residues of that RADA accent that I had been cultivating to get me through things in England. It didn't go down well and I was given a hard time in the backblocks. Darwin and the Northern Territory was rugged country. It wasn't dissimilar to India — you were travelling huge distances on a bus to get from any one place to another.

I finally got to Sydney and it was a little bit more civilised, but I didn't feel instantly at home. So I decided to carry on to New Zealand. I had sent some money ahead to a bank there so I knew I could manage for a while and have a good look around. When I got there I still looked like a hippie, but it didn't seem to bother people nearly so much, which was encouraging.

On the plane to Auckland I got talking to the passenger next to me, a travelling salesman who had been on holiday in England. I told him I had friends I could look up in Mt Eden — which is where I still live today.

'Oh, that's an older suburb,' he said. It turned out he lived in the relatively new suburb of Pakuranga. We kept talking and eventually he invited me to stay with him.

'I'll put you up for the night. Come back to our place and we'll give you something to eat and in the morning you can go and find your friends. My wife's meeting me at the airport.'

We got off the plane, and what he didn't know was that his father and mother had come up from Christchurch and arrived at about the same time. So they were in the car, their luggage was in the boot and his suitcase now had to go on their lap. I had two rucksacks and there was no way we were going to get everything in the car.

'Thanks for the offer,' I said, 'but I'm okay. I can make my own way.'

'No, no,' he said. 'It's fine.'

So they shuffled everything around and eventually we drove off to Pakuranga with him and his father holding my rucksacks out the windows.

That's when I realised that for Kiwis the impossible is the starting point — they work it out from there.

We went to his house and the next day when I woke up they had all gone to work. On the table were car keys, some money and a note that said: 'See you later tonight.'

The irony of that wonderful introduction to New Zealand is that, although you would expect us to have kept in touch, we didn't. I got myself organised quickly and within a couple of weeks I couldn't even remember his name.

My first mission was to get my hands on my money. Somebody had told me when we were travelling that the house prices in New Zealand had gone from $12,000 to $20,000 in a few years, which was why I had arranged for a few hundred thousand dollars to be put into a bank here.

The deal in those days was that if you sent money to an account, the account had to be used within a certain time —

you had to turn up and get it going. If not, it was sent back to its place of origin and it took another five days to get it sent back around the world again.

I had twenty cents of my own when I arrived, so was keen to get my money. I went to a bookshop, consulted a map to find out where my bank was and fronted up for my money.

I had missed the deadline.

'You've got no money,' I was told.

'What am I supposed to do?' I said. 'You've seen that I've got the money, so can you give me a cash advance just so I can go and get a bed for the night?'

'No, you have to wait five days.'

There was no arguing. The New Zealand girl from the bus had given me her family's phone number so I rang and stayed there on my second night.

I was still three days away from having any money when I saw a little poster ad that said 'Storeman/packer. Cash up front at the end of the day.'

It was for a Ramset company that made nuts and bolts. The job was just putting them in their boxes. I went along and because I could talk in whole sentences they said, 'We'll put you in dispatch. You send out the orders.'

I had a map of New Zealand, but I didn't know where any of the places that I was supposed to be sending things were. I had some rough ideas. I knew Mt Maunganui was a long way away and I knew Mt Eden wasn't a long way away. It went swimmingly for a while, and everything got dispatched on time. But after a couple of days, deliveries started coming back because I was doing things like sending a consignment by air to Mt Wellington. This was just across town in Auckland, but I had assumed if that was the mountain's name it must be in Wellington.

SMALL PRACTICALITIES ASIDE, New Zealand felt like nirvana from the moment I arrived. It was England without the Poms. For the most part. One exception was the white line up the middle of Queen Street. You were supposed to walk on the left-hand side. I was walking on the wrong side with my rucksack when a big guy, about six foot tall, but wearing walk shorts and white socks and sandals, which was a sight I was still getting used to, saw me and said, 'Walk on the left.'

I soon had my money and bought a villa in Mt Eden. By another stroke of luck, the New Zealand girl from the bus turned out to have an uncle who built harpsichords, flutes and all sorts of other musical instruments. He had a garage full of woodworking machinery and he taught me how to make things out of wood, and how to bend and shape it.

I got a lathe and made things to teach myself how to do mortise and tenon joints, laminate, and do embossing. My chemistry knowledge came into play, and I made my own antique stains and French polish.

I got stuck into renovating my wooden house. I had been brought up in brick houses, where the most you could do was cut a hole in a wall.

My house needed repiling. The old piles were made of heart rimu, bits of four by four. You might have been able to turn them into chair legs, but there wasn't much else you could do with them. However, it was great timber so I started laminating the pieces together into kitchen items, such as knife blocks.

I sold these to friends but eventually that turned into a business, called Rahh Design, which produced designer furniture and soft furnishings. The Scandinavian look was starting to take over from the old cottage style and I could make things that had the look people wanted — futuristic-looking coffee tables and so on.

The demand grew so much that I went into partnership with a local boatbuilder turned cabinetmaker. We both worked from our garages. He worked in his and I worked in mine, but his was much bigger than mine and he had a fully fledged workshop.

By now I was working during the day full-time at the Auckland University medical school. At night I came home and stayed in the workshop until midnight. I liked the precision of doing it and also playing with a long piece of wood and making a big coffee table and keeping the joints square. You felt strong, and it was nice not to have to think.

I eventually sold the business to my partner because I couldn't keep it up. He ran it for another fifteen years before the market all went to particle board and nobody wanted to buy solid furniture any more. They wanted veneer.

You're not a New Zealander until you've got your own nail gun. There are times today, trying to make something happen in Nepal or Eritrea, when all those skills I used building up that business come back into play. Not much knowledge gets wasted.

I was always learning. I had a big old television in the garage and the sound had failed, so I wired it to a portable radio for a speaker, soldered on the right connections and got the thing working. Finally the old cathode ray tube blew up, and it needed to be put out in the inorganic rubbish. I couldn't heft the whole thing because it was so big, so I chipped off the case and took off the base, but I was still left with the tube, which was connected by a big rubber bit that disappeared into the rest of the workings.

I got my garden secateurs, which of course weren't insulated, and I cut it. The tube contained 200,000 volts so whatever hair I had was suddenly sticking up and I found myself around the corner of the house feeling quite nice. Between that and the nitric acid explosion and the motorbike accident I have been lucky with my near misses.

I was lucky, too, to end up at university where I established a new SOP of forming a family of people to work on a big project. This was repeated many times over the years. I already had one small job at the School of Medicine which meant they knew about me and I was in the right place at the right time when they wanted to set up a Department of Clinical Pharmacology.

We didn't have a model because there wasn't one for pharmacology at the University of Auckland. We found a whole teaching course that was available from the University of Aberdeen and imported that.

Practical classes were a big part of it, and although I was never a formal lecturer I used to help design and run these.

Our course included a section that required us to anaesthetise salmon. You did that, brought them around again with your antidote and measured how long it took. This called for a stock of 500 salmon to be maintained, which would have been fine in Aberdeen but was out of the question here. It would have cost us a fortune.

Instead we went out to the Mt Roskill pet fish supply store and bought all the goldfish we needed.

But back in class I calculated the anaesthetic dose based on what was right for a 2kg salmon instead of a 50g goldfish. When we gave them the drug they went to sleep and floated to the surface, dead.

We needed to get rid of them and thought the simplest way was to flush them down the toilet. It needed several toilets, but we did it and went on with our other work.

I was back in my office when I heard screaming coming from the women's toilets. The anaesthetic had leached out when it got diluted in the water. Some of the fish had revived and were jumping up and down in the toilet bowls.

As well as running teaching classes the department set up a leading-edge pharmaceutical research unit. One of our most notorious clinical trials was a study of the effect of alcohol on T and B cell antibodies — the cells that attack cancer cells.

The hypothesis was that alcohol weakened the effect of human T and B cells, which was particularly bad for people with cancer. It was a proper trial to be written up in a reputable medical journal. We had to get clinical approval from the University Ethics Committee because it involved getting volunteers to drink an inordinate amount of alcohol.

The experiment was done on people who didn't have cancer, because whether you have it or not the effect on T and B cells will be the same. We used vodka because it gave you the weakest hangover. We got masses of it and diluted it 50/50 with orange juice and people were allowed to imbibe it as they would at a party.

About twenty subjects took part, most of them people from within the department and a few students. We hadn't really thought it through.

I was supervising taking blood samples, and I wasn't quite a nurse but the theory was that if we let people consume whatever they wanted we would get a good spread of alcohol concentrations. Then we would know, for instance, whether people who were totally legless were any worse off than someone who'd had just a couple of glasses. How much alcohol did it take to make a difference, if any?

Well, all of the trial participants just got completely trolleyed. It was human nature in the raw, and I was struggling to keep the trial alive. I was struggling even to find the buggers. There were people going out for a piss and not coming back. They just wandered off.

There was an attractive secretary in the department who I came across when I was looking for my missing volunteers. She was typing away but when I looked closer, one of the department academics had his head in her lap and was telling her how much he loved her.

A scientific paper was eventually published and the trial summary concluded that alcohol depressed your T and B cells quite significantly.

I was the head technical officer of the department, and the equivalent of *MASH*'s Radar O'Reilly. I could get you anything: space, equipment, funding for international travel. I was the man, but I was a benevolent benefactor. I was seen as a nice chap who helped everybody out. I was very keen on building the department and making it successful.

The technical staff in general were regarded as men and women of the world compared with the academics and the medicos. The latter were at the top of the hierarchy, then came academics and then the technical staff. So it was unusual for a technical officer to have his office next to that of the department head. This reflected the contribution I made to the day-to-day running of the department. It functioned well and we had more revenue than any other department in the university because, using my analytical chemistry background, I had established a drug-testing unit for conducting bio-equivalence studies on generic drugs for private companies.

It took about three years of hard work to get the department running as a world-class teaching and research unit and I enjoyed the time immensely. I loved the gentleness and camaraderie of academic life and the family we made there. The dean of the medical school at that time was an amateur wood turner and I set up a twice-yearly arts event where people who dabbled in art for a hobby brought their work and displayed it.

I started a film club and a weekly staff social club. We couldn't sell alcohol in those days but we could sell tickets that you exchanged for alcohol. After enough alcohol, people started to integrate. One film night we were changing reels when we saw on the screen these silhouettes and shadows of two people making unmistakable movements. They got a standing ovation.

Colleagues came camping with me on Great Barrier Island for long weekends and we had proper relationships. I was making the world the way I wanted it to be.

THE PERSON I WAS closest to at university was Phil Brown. He joined as a technician and went on to become a senior technician, running all the clinical trial work. He was from England, had very good qualifications and was probably smarter than me. But he was also very vulnerable and I sensed that. I befriended him and he became my best friend for about fourteen years. We were as close as you could be in terms of brotherly love.

We came in every morning, sorted out what needed to be done and then went down the road for a coffee. And we were highly competitive.

We were a good team. Part of our job was to buy equipment and set up other teaching labs. For this we dealt with a sales rep, concluding deals for tens of thousands of dollars' worth of glassware. We made it compulsory that he had to come at lunchtime and play darts with us.

Phil was a darts expert and he got his dartboard set up in the teaching lab downstairs and we played darts. In the course of that we filled the guy up with grog. Then we did the deal. We could save $10,000 or $20,000 in an hour by getting him legless.

We had a joint relationship with a university in Kyoto. One of their researchers, Professor Kazu Kurahasi, had been working with us in Auckland on drugs to stop arrhythmia in heart tissue. For this we had to do real Boris Karloff stuff involving cutting rats' hearts out, stringing them up, causing chemical-induced arrhythmia and recording heartbeats in real time.

Eventually we all transferred to Kyoto to continue the research. Phil and I were to go for between three and six months to help set up his lab. During the day we did that and at night we became indoctrinated into the Japanese way of life, which I loved for its serenity and aesthetic sense.

Phil was not quite so keen — he was a ham and cheese sandwich man who struggled with the food in particular.

Our evening SOP was a pub crawl with our colleagues. We played Jenka — a fairground-type game of chance played with balls. Workers wanting to unwind would stand around smoking copiously while they poured hundreds of dollars into this game for the chance to win trivial prizes like cigarettes.

Then we went to bars, but in a specific order. We began with the one where our friend first used to go when he was at university. There were geisha girls, which meant no hanky-panky, although their job was to make sure your glass stayed filled. They were beautiful and elegant and seemed to be able to produce anything from cigarette lighters to combs from within their voluminous kimonos.

Then the drinking got more serious, with a kamikaze spirit as you worked your way through whisky or sake.

Once we were in a bar where a woman produced little round snacks that looked like Maltesers with shells made of rice paper. This bar served giant two-litre jugs of beer. I reached out and grabbed one of these tasty snacks and it erupted into what felt like fermenting elephant snot — it was all I could do not to vomit. I threw half of the beer down and that got rid of most of the taste. Phil had been talking with someone and not seen my reaction, so I passed the bowl over.

'Phil, have one of these, they're really good.'

Now Phil was very prone to vomiting. In fact, he was a sympathetic vomiter, who would throw up if he saw anyone else throw up out in the street. When he bit into the snack, he leapt up and ran through the door. We could hear him trying to pass his lower intestine through his mouth.

Drinking games were a compulsory part of Japanese social life. One of the most popular was to fill a sake vessel to the brim until a meniscus appeared — the dome shape liquids form on the surface before they spill. Then you went around the group adding a drop at a time. The person whose drop overflowed the cup had to drink the lot. It was a slippery slope to oblivion because once you got a little bit pissed there was no way you could control the drops.

I had some advantages — more body weight than the locals and a lifetime of training in labs filling containers with liquids to precise measurements. I was a meniscus maestro.

The poshest bar ever was at the end of a night with Kazu's father-in-law, an impressive character in his seventies, who was the head of a sake manufacturing plant. Here there were the A-list geisha girls, wearing garments and playing instruments that were centuries old. You didn't go there every night, but perhaps once a month. Here we learnt how to eat horse meat, which was reputedly a source of strength. That also got you pissed because you had to swallow so much alcohol just to keep it down.

As we walked home down a narrow alleyway, our gaits revealed our varying stages of inebriation. The old boy walked straight ahead like a man on a mission. Kazu looked like he was on a bit of string, weaving from side to side but hitting the walls. Behind him was Phil who looked like he was on a yoyo — staggering from side to side and bouncing off the walls. And I brought up the rear, so pissed that at one stage I tried to look behind to see if I was doing the same thing.

Generally, behaviour in Japan was more civilised and serene. I could easily have lived in this highly structured, polite society with its beautiful rituals and exquisite temples. I had a great sense of peace while there. I spent a lot of time studying the architecture and ended up building a scale model of a temple, using no nails, in my garden.

Also, at home in New Zealand when I got invited places my hosts always tried to invite a single woman in the hope something long-term might develop. In Japan, the sexes don't socialise together, so I didn't have that pressure.

DURING THESE FIRST YEARS in New Zealand I had been living with an English girl who had been on the bus, and who I loved dearly because she was the gentlest of souls. We moved in together when I was renovating the house and we had scientific interests in common — she was a biochemist, doing fundamental research at Greenlane Hospital.

Over the next few years, she became very interested in naturopathy and our paths began to diverge. She went on long-weekend touch-for-health events. All my friends from the medical school were career alcoholics. They came around to the house for a meal and plenty of wine while she looked on, appalled that we were poisoning our bodies.

No meat was kept in the house. After a time all we had in the fridge was horse-shit smoothies — brown drinks containing everything but animal products, which tasted terrible.

It became obvious things weren't going to last. One turning point was a group of her friends that came round, who had been out for a picnic on Bethells Beach, and one of them was explaining that they had met somebody extraterrestrial on the beach. I realised that either I was mad or they were. The final straw for me was that every morning I had to see the wet colonic irrigation set hanging behind the door, and I thought, 'If I turn my back, it's going to rape me.'

We didn't stay together — not because we didn't love each other but because we no longer wanted to go in the same direction. She had given me great love and was instrumental in bringing me to New Zealand.

I have never regretted settling in New Zealand. The very notion has never occurred to me. There was so much to like. I count myself so lucky that I stumbled on this place, because I couldn't have done the stuff I do anywhere else. We had a saying in England that somebody who was out there and ready to give things a go had 'more front than Sainsbury's', the big supermarket, and that is how I found New Zealanders. They all had more front than Sainsbury's.

In England, everyone, everything and everywhere was the same. I spent years living in rows and rows of terrace houses. On the corner of one, occasionally, there was a newsagent, with a pub on the other corner. They probably built the houses around the pub. The person living in 12A didn't go anywhere except to the newsagent or the pub. Life was very regimented, and it had to be with the sheer volume of people that needed to move around. Going on the train, going on the bus, back and forth every day.

When I took a girl home to her house it was a two-up and two-down terrace. You went in the front door and there was the lounge and out the back was the kitchen and upstairs were two bedrooms that opened to a bathroom. When you went to visit them, you sat in the middle of the settee with the girlfriend, and her parents sat in chairs on either side watching television. Then it was time to go home.

Some terrace rows had a small narrow lane that wasn't a full road width but enough for a small truck to go along to collect the rubbish. If you walked up these at the end of a Friday or Saturday night, you found condoms discarded in the lane. People just banged each other against the wall because there was nowhere else.

There is an old joke about some Australians and some Poms landing on an island populated by beautiful girls. The Australians start fighting over the girls but the Poms don't. They stand there waiting to be introduced. You can't initiate anything in England. You have to wait to be asked.

New Zealand couldn't be more different. Information is shared. It's an open-source country. In England, the plumber always comes with a mate and the first thing they do is light the gas to make themselves a cup of tea. In New Zealand a plumber once turned up at my house, had a look at my problem and said, 'You don't really need me. I can show you how to fix that.'

All nirvana. I hate institutions because of how I was brought up, so I have an absolute antipathy to being told what to do or being regulated. In New Zealand there is comparatively little regulation and things are much more negotiable than they are in a lot of other countries.

In the UK there is segregation in terms of north and south, and people up north hate the people down south. The Welsh hate the English, the Scots hate the English. In general, they're not a can-do race.

I have read all about the days of the charge of the Light Brigade or fighting the Zulus. The soldiers just stood there stoically and died. The British need to be told what to do before they do something. If nobody tells you that you can run away, you stay and get shot. The relationship between the troops was quite different with the Anzacs. We saw that in Anzac Cove where the Anzacs didn't want to be controlled by the Poms.

Still, when I arrived and wanted to build my holiday home on Great Barrier, which I never got around to building, I wanted to make sure I did everything right.

'Who does the building permits?' I asked one of the residents.

'The local police,' he said. 'You have to take the plans in and they do the approval.'

I saw the cop and told him I would get my architect to provide some plans.

'Nah, you don't need to do that. You are going to build it out of permanent materials, aren't you, not tea tree?'

'Yeah, tanalised pine.'

'You don't need tanalised, just four by two. Macrocarpa is fine.'

I told someone I had bought the cop a crate of beer to thank him. He told me a crate was too much. I had just inflated the rate for building permits.

SEVEN

The chemistry set

In line with my own personal SOP, having done all I could at
the university, I was looking for something new to do. Instead,
it found me in the person of a brilliant entrepreneur called Sir
Graeme Douglas, who is one of the retail giants who inspired
me over the years. He still does. He started out with a couple
of local pharmacies which grew into a multi-million-dollar
international pharmaceutical business. And he did it against all
odds, with multinationals trying to stop him at every turn.

At the university we had been doing a lot of clinical trial
work for Graeme, who wanted everything of the very highest
standard. In pharmaceuticals that means if, for instance, you are
going to launch a new paracetamol tablet, you have to compare
it with the existing market leader by doing a double-blind

trial that compares the clinical absorption rates and clinical effectiveness and so on. This independent testing was very important for Graeme's products to be accepted by the New Zealand Department of Health.

One day Graeme came to see me.

'I want you to come and work for me to set up the Douglas pharmaceutical division,' he said. 'I've got a few products which are not subject to international patents and I want to set up my own pharmaceutical manufacturing facility.'

He wanted to make generic drugs. That meant taking an existing product whose patent had expired, working out what was in it and making a version that was as good. It might not have the big international brand name, but it could be sold for a lot less than big international prices.

Patents on drugs typically run for twenty years, at which time you can apply for an extension. It gets complicated, because there were cases where we could start working on a drug even while it was under patent, and then other cases where what we could do depended on the country of origin and its laws.

The big companies could bend the rules by saying, with something very successful and profitable, that although the patent was up, several of these years had been used getting the product to market through quality studies and trials. Therefore, they had not been able to make money off it for much of the patent period — even though they might have made many times more than they expected to make, in the shorter time the drug was on the market. So they claimed, and sometimes got, an extension.

I was enthusiastic about what I saw as important and worthwhile work, because internationally the drug companies were artificially inflating the prices of life-saving drugs, putting them out of reach of many people in the developed world, let alone those in the developing world. We showed there could be alternatives. It's a lesson I took to the developing world later.

The job suited me because I could, probably for the first time in my life, use the combination of my analytical chemistry skills, my management skills and my entrepreneurial skills.

We were doing product realisation, although we didn't know that was what we were doing. Product realisation is when you know exactly who you are going to sell the product to and how you are going to sell it. To some degree that was already done for us because there was an existing market and an existing product. We just had to make — or realise — the product.

Graeme took me out to Stoddard Road in Mt Roskill and he showed me this big factory space.

'Build me a state-of-the-art quality assurance testing laboratory and a pharmaceutical manufacturing plant,' he said.

So I collared my friend Phil Brown and took him out there with a piece of chalk and we started to draw lines on the floor and argue about what could or should go where.

It was a condition of my going to work for Graeme that I could bring Phil with me if he wanted to come. I needed my number one man to look after things and watch my back. Graeme was fine with that. I was technical manager for the company and Phil was manager of the quality assurance division. He got on well with people and I was able to leave a lot of day-to-day stuff to Phil.

With our variety of experience we had a big combined knowledge base. We researched how standard pharmaceutical plants were being built around the world and realised there was a lot that could be improved. We looked at things like how we could use the construction of the plant to reduce microbiological contamination. We looked at different options for people flow as products moved through the production cycle. In summary, we took the best of the known technology for making multi-product pharmaceuticals and made it better.

I found two new families at Douglas. The first was Graeme and his wife, Ngaire, to both of whom I became close. In the early days of building the head office, Ngaire and I even went out to choose the furniture together. I worked ten hours a day, seven days a week during the commissioning of the factory and headquarters. It was not unusual on Saturday mornings, when I was on site on my own, for Ngaire and Graeme to bring fish and chips and for us to sit on the loading dock of the half-finished building having lunch.

Douglas Pharmaceuticals is a family company and Graeme is an absolute gentleman, a throwback to Wye College if anything. He has a dignified aura about him that isn't off-putting, and every few days he took a turn around the factory to let everyone know how important their work was and keep up a spirit of camaraderie. He continues to do this, twenty-five years later.

Ngaire is the mother I never had. She is an extraordinary, intelligent and elegant woman with an exemplary sense of fair play and style, but her real talent is to disarm people with her exquisite sense of humour and adventure. She and I had great fun choosing the furniture for Graeme's office and then going off for a meal at the Top of the Town restaurant.

One day we were having lunch and one of the waiters whispered in her ear, 'Mrs Douglas, I thought you may wish to know that Mr Douglas has made a booking at the restaurant and will be arriving in about twenty minutes.'

Ngaire shrieked with delight. 'He thinks we are having an affair.' We laughed with the abandon of children. That is the special magic of Ngaire Douglas. She made my world very beautiful.

ONCE WE GOT THE manufacturing facility up and running, the analytical detective work to produce quality generic drugs started.

One big component of Graeme's vision was that, as well as being a very ethically focused company, we had an unrelenting commitment to doing everything to world-class standards.

For one thing, that was to protect us from multinationals finding fault and saying our generic drugs weren't as good as their proprietary ones.

So I was working not only to build the pharmaceutical manufacturing facilities but also to set up all the quality systems. We ended up with the best quality system in the world, because we redesigned everything. We took all the quality systems for all the companies we could find information on, and found ways to make them even better. We wrote hundreds of SOPs to very high standards. Everybody was committed to that.

When you are working with drugs, there are unique occupational safety and health issues to consider. We were making penicillin products and some people are allergic to penicillin, so you had to make sure they were screened before they went into these areas. And we were making drugs that had steroids in them, so you didn't want your chief tablet-maker Doug to turn into Denise. We had morphine for hospitals and you didn't want people accidentally consuming it, so we had a lot of stringent legal controls around who we employed.

A good example of our work was our version of the asthma drug Ventolin, which was selling for around $58. We created a version that could sell for $18. Ironically, in some cases our products were so good and so well priced that the multinationals ended up ceasing to do their own production and contracting us to do it for them.

We weren't always about cutting costs. For hospitals we

developed an alternative to fiddly bottles for dispensing pills. We put them in plastic reels so they could be torn off as needed.

My various experiences were feeding into a whole pool of knowledge — technical drawing, art, garden design, plus all the chemistry I had learnt and developed at the Department of Pharmacology — which meant I could take on challenging tasks with confidence. We made Douglas a leading-edge pharmaceutical company over about seven years.

At our peak we were back engineering — taking an existing item and then working out how it was made — about a product a week. There were two ways of breaking down an existing product and reconstructing it. The first was to go to a reference book or to the original patent which was now off patent and see if you could learn something through that. As a strategy, it wasn't necessarily successful because often they changed their formulas over the years.

The best thing to do was the second method: go to a shop, grab a box of the stuff off the shelf and find out what was in it. For me that was wonderful, because it was everything I was trained to do, going back to the analytical testing laboratory days. If you give me four technicians, a UV spectrophotometer, IR spectrophotometer and High Performance Liquid Chromatograph (HPLC) machine, I can tell you what is in pretty much anything in less than a day.

In my years at South-Eastern Laboratories in Canterbury we did not have sophisticated equipment, so we used gravimetric analysis — basic chemical reactions — to determine what was in things. To measure viscosity you took your substance, put it on the window and recorded how fast and how far it ran down. So I had a pragmatic approach to product realisation and all the high-tech equipment just added to my armoury of analytical skills. I could probably pick up a cosmetic formula and tell you what was in it, or at least identify the emulsifying agent, by feeling it and rubbing it in.

We worked out the components of these things, right down to whether it was polysorbate 60 or polysorbate 80, and then I said to the technicians, 'It doesn't really matter. Their physical and chemical properties are nearly identical and we're confident when we do a clinical trial that this will be absorbed at the same rate as that.'

But the lesson about doing things to the highest possible standards had been drummed into these guys so well that once I went home and came back in the morning to find they had been up all night just so they could say triumphantly: 'It's polysorbate 80.'

They were so proud of themselves.

It was the family atmosphere that kept people working like that. There were no bosses. Everybody was allowed to express their personalities. Obviously, I wasn't going to work anywhere that stifled people's individuality or institutionalised them.

I set up the framework for a good co-operative culture and everyone had to comply with it. No one was going to be allowed to climb to the top over the backs of their colleagues. One of the management rules I instituted was the Superman rule. We had weekly management meetings between the heads of the Production and Quality Assurance and Regulatory Affairs departments. The Superman rule was simple and elegant: if anyone started going on about their or their department's achievements, rather than acting as part of the team, then anyone could put their hand in the air and mimic Superman taking off, with suitable accompanying whooshing noises. Egos were left at the door and a collegiate management group emerged.

Other rituals developed. Whenever we cracked the code for

a drug, Phil pretended he was on a horse and rode his invisible mount right around the floor, cracking an imaginary whip and yelling, 'Hi ho, Silver.' I followed and eventually the whole R&D team joined in. Everyone in production thought we were nuts.

Not every formula was perfect and we had a phrase for that: 'Fruito Fizz', which originated from an old *Only Fools and Horses* episode where they bought some canned fruit and it had gone off and fermented. They sold it as Fruito Fizz because it was fizzy.

One day, my colleague Ian Hickling, who would later come to Eritrea with me to work on the Hollows lens plant, had made a lotion. You check the stability of the product by putting it in a fridge and an incubator alternately. If the oil and water parts separate, that means the emulsion is not strong enough and the product will fail in the marketplace. Ian had been working all night on the hydrocortisone equivalent formula.

'Look, it's fucked,' he said. He shook it and a bit splashed on the desk and made it shine.

'Shit, Fruito Fizz,' said Phil, and he started polishing his desk with it. We all laughed, but the next morning it had crystallised and it was like there had been a snow fall on Phil's desk.

By the end of my years at Douglas, where we had started with Graeme's few basic products, we had produced 167 different drugs — although that figure includes several we produced in various potencies. We counted those variants because each had to go through the same series of clinical trials as the others for US Food and Drug Administration approval.

We made everything from steroids to penicillin-type products, liquids and creams, tablets, capsules, and some medical devices. I went in with a lot of knowledge, but I ended up knowing an awful lot more about pharmaceutical manufacturing and building pharmaceutical plants.

MY ROMANTIC SIDE, after the opportunities I had made the most of at medical school were no longer there, went into a decline. I had a lot of female friends, who weren't necessarily lovers, and the occasional fling, but nothing major.

Typically, I worked until about six or seven o'clock, then I went home with documents and paperwork that I went over in front of the tele. I cooked my dinner and had a couple of whiskies and either kept doing paperwork until midnight or went to work on a painting. I had a room set aside as a studio and I kept making art for a long time.

Once I met a woman and invited her to dinner, definitely thinking there would be more than dinner happening, but before she arrived I had picked up my brush and got engrossed in a picture. I was absolutely captured by it. I love painting because it completely absorbs me and everything else goes away. Dinner never happened, or anything else.

Painting was the ultimate mistress and that is why I decided to give it up altogether because it was so demanding it was hard to maintain a balance between it and everything else.

For most of the time at Douglas I didn't have anyone to go home to — the offices were my home. I went in at the weekend to work, and I wasn't the only one. A lot of the others were scientists who didn't have much interest in girlfriends, so they came in and we worked on projects. The business was growing so much there was always something to do.

So most of my relationships at the time were more like family ones, with colleagues at Douglas. There was an analytical chemist, who was a rather attractive female, who was married. She had worked for me at the medical school, then come to work at Douglas and we had grown up together to some degree. I felt very comfortable with her and she felt very comfortable with me.

I would go down to the laboratory when she was working on a machine and put my arms around her and put my head on her shoulder and give her a hug. That was just how it was and that's all it was.

Every time we cracked a formula or had another reason to celebrate we had a party. And because these people were my family I liked to nurture them. I cooked meals for them, which they probably didn't like because I was into Japanese food then, and they probably wanted fish and chips. But they tolerated it, and some of our late-night meals went on until one or two in the morning.

We had competitions between the scientists and the people in production. We were the nerds with pens in our pocket protectors, and they were the ones who went out playing rugby at the weekend, so we were useless, especially at indoor cricket, which was what we usually played. Whenever we dived for a ball we seemed to just get tangled up in the net, but we always gave it our best shot. The day we actually beat them for once we thought we were the best thing ever.

When you have an atmosphere like that and get close to the people you work with things can get a little loose. It's as though the more demanding you are and the higher the professional standards you set, the more you need to let off steam in other ways.

I was in a very important meeting with clients once when we were renovating the whole factory. We couldn't use the boardroom, so we were squeezed into the small staff tearoom. The visitors had their backs to the door, and I sat opposite, facing the door. I was in the middle of the presentation when my friend who used to let me have a hug when I needed one came in. She stood in the door and lifted up her skirt to give me an eyeful. I had to sit there as if nothing unusual was happening.

Although we were nerds we had visitors who were even nerdier. There were regular visits from a collaborating university researcher who always had a pocket protector in his shirt, containing at least six pens. I arrived late at one of these meetings to find all of my team had all got pocket protectors and filled them with at least ten pens.

In the very early days at Douglas, I had a staff photo taken once a year. I am there trying to look distinguished and as though I am still at Wye College, but there are people getting up to all sorts of stuff in the background. One woman is pretending to strangle me — another is making rabbit ears behind people. And that ended up being the most sensible picture we could get.

I had created a team that reflected my core values: work harder than everyone else, with great passion and diligence, love each other, make quality your bible in everything you do, and just be yourself. I like the fact that these scientists did not perceive me as the big white chief and felt comfortable enough on any given day to take the piss out of me to my face.

But if I asked them to, and I often did, they would follow me to hell and back and then jump alongside Phil and say, 'Hi ho, Silver.'

Sir Graeme Douglas seemed to float above all this. He had a special kind of dignity that nothing could penetrate — even when serious attempts were made.

Once, some of us were in a meeting with a rep who was trying to sell us a contraceptive sponge for women. He also had some condoms he wanted us to license the technology for. Graeme's practice was to come to the first part of these meetings and then leave while the details were being sorted out.

While he was there, the rep talked about the sponge and we discussed whether there were going to be regulatory issues with the Health Department and whether women — and men —

would accept a vaginal sponge and be prepared to use it.

After Graeme had gone the rep brought out his condoms. Condoms have a spermicidal lubricant called Nonoxynol 9 which is very effective but both smells and tastes awful.

'This Nonoxynol 9 is highly purified and doesn't have that taste,' said the rep. And he had us all licking these condoms so we could see they didn't taste too bad. At that point Graeme returned because he had forgotten something and was confronted by the sight of a roomful of his employees sitting around a table licking condoms.

'Gentlemen, I'm not going to ask,' he said, and left the room.

THROUGHOUT THE COMBINED mayhem and seriousness, Phil and I remained best friends.

When we were discussing a problem, he was always doing something absent-minded with his hands, like making paper planes. My room overlooked the factory floor, which was why it often ended up with paper planes littered everywhere.

He had an old-style compass with a pencil on one arm and spike on the other that he used to jab into his desk. I knew it was going to end up in his leg long before he did. He was also one of those people who tip their chair back on its rear legs. Once, during an important conference call to the US, he leant back too far and ended up on the floor. All I could see across the table were his legs in the air, but he carried on the conversation lying on his back.

We were very happy at work and we were extraordinarily well paid, receiving huge bonuses from the dollars that were coming into the company. We were as close as brothers could be, so when he killed himself, it was devastating.

I was at work one morning when I got a call from the police.

'Do you have a car, registered to Douglas Pharmaceuticals?' the cop said and he quoted a licence plate number.

'Yes, I do.'

'Who was driving that car?'

I knew it was Phil's car. 'Has there been an accident?'

'Who are you?' asked the cop.

'I'm Ray Avery, the technical director and a friend of Phil's as well.'

'We found him down at Muriwai Beach last night. He committed suicide. The car's ready for collection and the good news is he hadn't soiled the car and you can pick it up.'

I was numb. You don't know what to do or who to tell. I had learned from an early age to keep a rein on my emotions so there was no breaking down or losing control. But the emotions were there. I was bereft.

I had to tell Graeme and everyone else, including Ian Hickling. I said, 'Phil's committed suicide.' Ian was as bereft as I was. We went down the road to the local pub and sat there and just looked at each other. There was nothing to say. Eventually I went back, got on the blower and phoned around to tell everybody what had gone on.

In our conversations together over the years, Phil and I had talked about everything and anything. One day as pharmaceutical scientists we had speculated about suicide and what the best, least painful way to do it would be. We settled on a drug that would stop your heart, but that is very painful, so we thought you should also take another drug that would put you to sleep before the fatal one kicked in. And we decided whisky and coke was the best vehicle for taking them.

I knew a little about forensic examination sites from my years at South-Eastern Laboratories. When I went to get the car the police had taken all the pills, and there would have been a lot of them because Phil always had lots of different drugs that were for work lying around his car. But there was an empty Coke bottle left on the floor.

I guess I was trying to give the story some sort of ending when I put what was left in the bottle into our HPLC machine to analyse. Sure enough, it was the Phil/Ray cocktail.

There had been no sign. No warning. I knew Phil was having problems at home but we had never really talked about it. Men don't. Every day he rocked up and sat with me. We used to stand looking out the window together, never needing to say anything in particular. I just enjoyed being with such a delightfully gentle and caring person.

I think the biggest tragedy of my life was that Phil didn't survive. He would have loved the work we do now and would have been a great member of the band of brothers that formed around our later efforts in Eritrea and Nepal.

I'm not sure, but I think I got rid of all the grief I had with Phil when I was driving up to Whangarei some time later. I was driving through a small town on a beautiful sunny day, not thinking about anything particularly when I looked across and saw a park. Its name was the same as Phil's surname. I stopped the car right in the middle of the road and I cried my heart out. Cars had to drive around me. People came up to the car to find out what was wrong, saw me crying and freaked out and took off. I stayed there for I don't know how long.

It wasn't just about Phil, it was also about what had happened with Graeme when he hanged himself at school. Having that happen to a close friend once was one thing, but a second time was almost beyond belief. I hadn't had that many close friends. And it was about everything else that had happened to me. The whole world came crashing down at that point. All I could think was, 'What's the point?' Even now, when I had the nice life from Claridge's window and the family that I had made to replace the one my parents didn't give me, and all the money I could ever need — it could all be made worthless in an instant.

It went on for a while. That was the only time in my life I ever let go.

I carried on at work but it was never going to be the same. About a week later, I was standing looking out the window where Phil and I used to stand together having our coffee every morning. All of a sudden there was the sound of crying. I turned around and it was one of the technicians we had worked with for years. She had got a shock because she was so used to seeing us there together.

The Douglas Pharmaceuticals family took a terrible collective blow from Phil's death.

I had been there about six years, and my interest was waning. When you have done something several times, there is nothing more to discover. I didn't want to carry on doing the same things without Phil's company. In a way, his death gave me my freedom. The business was under control and running smoothly. All the SOPs were in place. Other people I was close to had left and if I'd stayed I would have had to build a whole new family. Besides, we were getting to a point where the family was so large that you couldn't have those personalised relationships anyway. I became more like a public relations consultant in dealing with unions and so on.

I ran the risk of getting what I call the freezing works syndrome. Freezing workers go on strike — or did in those days — for more money, but it's not because they actually want more money. It's because the job's shitty. Some people invoke change by packing a sad and having a fight with their boss so they get sacked. They haven't got enough guts to do it themselves.

I also felt at some level that because Phil didn't get to have a full crack at life, I needed to make the most of mine. Just blobbing around would have been a different kind of wasted life.

I recognised all of that and decided to make a strategic exit and take the knowledge I had learnt and use it in another way.

WHICH IS HOW I came to create the Kaizen Group. I had a whole library of intellectual property which I could use that really wasn't covered by the IP of Douglas or anybody else. Kaizen was a company formed to set up best-practice pharmaceutical plants around the world. They didn't have to be big ones but I could give smaller companies the benefit of big-company knowledge and techniques. It meant these countries could get quality drugs manufactured for a much lower price than the imported versions.

We helped them to get product realisation files, so they could register drugs with the FDA. We provided a one-stop shop: 'We will build your plant and show you how to make your stuff and help you design the products right down to the packaging.' It was an exciting idea and it helped me get going again.

I knew I could do it from New Zealand, because I had Graeme Douglas's example before me: a retail pharmacist who started on a tiny scale and built a huge multi-million-dollar business using local talent and knowledge and creating a huge export industry.

It wasn't hard to find customers. In my work building plants with Douglas, which involved dealing with key people every step of the way, from air-conditioning engineers to lab equipment suppliers, I had come in contact with many potential clients. In fact, one firm approached me when I was still at Douglas to see if I would help them set up a plant in China. I was not interested at the time, but I knew there was a need for these skills out there.

I made it a virtual business. I didn't charge anything for doing my part of the job, but I took a cut of all the contractors' fees on the project. I did a floor plan in four or five days, then went to the site to make sure everything was being done to International Good Manufacturing Standards.

Kaizen did projects in China, Vietnam and India. The contractors worked directly for the client because I didn't want to be left holding the baby if someone in another country didn't pay their bill.

It was a good business because the total cost of the projects was high, which meant even a small percentage was a lot of money for not very much hands-on work.

Every now and then I got on a plane to check a job. I went around with a box of red stickers and a pen. If something wasn't right I put a sticker on it or marked it with the pen. Sometimes there was a lot of red, and I used to get asked if I didn't have any crayons when I was a kid.

Kaizen is a Japanese word that means 'constant', and it comes from a philosophy of constant improvement in life. I thought it was an ideal name because it symbolised what I was trying to do — constantly improve as a human being.

It is underpinned by a whole range of other ideas, such as that colleagues are also customers. That means, for example, if I am doing something on a production line and you are working next to me, you are not just another part of a production line, you are my customer. I have to provide you with a good product. I should have a respectful relationship with you, so I shouldn't give you the crap part and then blame you for something that comes out at the end. It's a way of making everybody work together.

When I started the company I thought that was what we wanted to sell to the clients, a philosophy of building quality into everything they do, and that way you can't lose. Now it underpins what I am trying to do in the developing world. There is no point making something the same as somebody else already makes, even if you make it cheaper. You might as well make something better.

The work brought me face to face with different business cultures in ways that were sometimes unexpected. When we were building a plant in Vietnam, the area where we were working was prone to flooding. Running through it were big waterways to deal with the flooding. Next to them were flat run-off areas. People had started to build houses on these, but the weight of the buildings made the waterways crack. So all the architects who had given permission for the building were taken out and shot.

Not good for the architects, but not great for us either, because it meant no one wanted to sign off on projects. We had a hell of a job getting the building permits through. Everybody was terrified they would get shot. In other countries we haven't really had any problems.

Kaizen also provided expert guidance on environmental controls for buildings, which is how we ended up making probably the biggest ostrich containment facility in the world. It was in the days when some New Zealanders thought ostriches were going to be the next big thing and a mini-ostrich-farming boom took place.

The birds were brought in from South Africa and were subject to strict quarantine. They couldn't be exposed to the

New Zealand ambient environment for six months. They had to come into the country in their own crate with their own air-conditioning system with their own High Performance particle arresting (HEPA) filter. It was bizarre to start with, then it got weirder. The plane had been delayed in Dubai for 18 hours on the tarmac in the hot sun and many of the birds died of heatstroke before they got here.

Those that made it were taken in individual trucks to the facility we made. They were driven inside, the doors were locked and that was it for six months.

And there was this one poor guy in there with them to look after them for six months. It was pre-cellphone. He had a fax machine and he could fax information back and forth. His wife used to come and see him through the glass.

It turned out ostriches produce a whole heap of nitrogen and ammonia and the air had to be recirculated, with very little air being dumped outside because it might have brought foreign contaminants into the New Zealand environment.

The ammonia built up. The guy got red eyes and so did the ostriches. We had to install an ammonia scrubbing plant very quickly. Meanwhile, ostriches started dying. The guy started putting the dead ones in the cool room but soon ran out of space and had to cut them up into smaller pieces with a chainsaw to fit them in the freezer. And eventually, of course, the ostrich boom never really happened and investors lost their money.

Kiwifruit were a lot less difficult to manage. We were looking into getting the fruit to ripen quicker by feeding them gas and controlling their environment.

I noticed that some of the kiwifruit packers were wearing gloves and some weren't. I asked if the gloves were because the fruit was prickly.

'No,' I was told. 'It's because the actinase enzyme in the fruit will eventually wear away your fingerprints.' This was a small seed of information that became vitally important later on and, in fact, will end up saving millions of infants' lives. Back then, though, I was just exercising normal scientific curiosity. Weren't the people without gloves worried about what would happen to their fingers?

'No, you get really soft skin.'

That was true too. Kiwifruit is a very effective exfoliant. Then I remembered the number of barbecues I had been to where I had been taught the New Zealand trick of leaving some kiwifruit on steak for a couple of hours to tenderise it before cooking.

Kiwifruit contains a potent protease enzyme. If you have a chicken at the right temperature and immerse it in kiwifruit pulp, you will find after about four hours that all you have left is the bones. You don't want to get it anywhere near your eyes because it will dissolve the proteins in them.

So, Kaizen became quite a diverse company able to do very different things, but always with an eye on best practice and ethical business. Some of what we learnt was by chance, as with the kiwifruit. We also had a great team who enjoyed working together and produced great results.

We had got as good as you can get at building world-class medical manufacturing facilities. And then I crossed paths with someone who needed help to build a world-class medical manufacturing facility — an Australian surgeon called Fred Hollows. And my life got turned around again.

EIGHT

Visionary

When I met Fred Hollows, I didn't think I would end up on this path. He wanted someone who knew what they were doing to go to Eritrea and help set up a plant to manufacture intraocular lenses — artificial lenses that can be transplanted into people's eyes to defeat cataract blindness and allow them to see. I thought it was going to be a simple job. I was going to do a few plans, knock up a factory. In the event, I found a whole new purpose to my life that sustains me to this day. But it took a fair bit of finding.

In 1992, Fred was in New Zealand, his home country, to launch the local branch of the Fred Hollows Foundation, which had been set up to help carry out his work. A friend thought I could help with setting up the labs and encouraged me to meet him.

I turned up at the Sheraton Hotel in Auckland, dressed in my How-do-you-do-Ray-Avery- CEO-of-the-Kaizen-Group suit, for what I thought was going to be a business meeting. But Fred was saying his goodbyes to family and friends because he was about six months away from dying of cancer. He had his trademark whisky with him, though. An old colleague from the medical school introduced me to Fred as a scientist who could build labs in Africa and Asia, but Fred, who usually made a point of being as rude as possible, didn't even acknowledge me.

'Yeah, but is he any bloody good?' he snorted and kept moving.

I gave it some thought, then took off after him and caught him by the arm.

'Fred, you're dying of cancer, they tell me,' I said, 'and I charge up to $1000 an hour in consultancy fees. Neither of us has much time to waste. Do you want to talk to me or not?'

'I like this guy, give him a whisky,' was Fred's response. So I had a whisky with him and we talked a little about his work, but he wasn't really here for that.

'Come to Sydney and have a proper bloody chat,' he said before going back to making his farewells.

Three weeks later I was in Sydney for business, and I caught up with Fred, his wife Gabi and the whole entourage. Fred laid out his plans.

'I've got all these things taken care of,' he said. 'Making the lenses is sorted. It's all written in stone. I've got this fantastic South African tool-maker who knows all about things.'

'Well, I can help you with quality controls for the lenses,' I said.

'Nah, it's all fucking taken care of, mate. Don't you worry about that. All I want is for you to look after the quality of the factory and make sure the building's all done.'

The background to what was really a very daring and creative plan was that Fred, who was an ophthalmologist, had a patient in Sydney who presented with a particular eye condition some years previously.

'Where are you from?' Fred asked.

'I am from Eritrea,' the man told him.

'Where's that?'

'In North Africa.'

'How many eye doctors have you got there?'

'I think we might have one.'

'That's terrible,' said Fred and he got on a plane and flew to Eritrea while the country was in the middle of a war with Ethiopia, fighting for its independence.

He began teaching the local doctors how to do good eye surgery. One day a group of them came to see him.

'Do you want to come and see our pharmaceutical manufacturing plant? It's in a cave up [in the mountains].'

'Christ,' said Fred, 'the last thing I want to do is go out in the middle of the night after a day's surgery to look at a couple of boxes of Aspro.'

But he went. The route was along a dried riverbed and there were a number of caves to visit. In the first they had tablet machines and were making pharmaceuticals. Everything had been moved to the safety of the caves and petrol generators had been brought in so they could continue to have medicines during the war.

There had even been a bunch of rabbits there for endotoxin testing, which is what you do to prove the medicines you've made are sterile and don't contain any pathogens. You inject a little bit of what you have made into the rabbit and monitor its temperature. If it goes up, then you have to throw the batch out.

That was remarkable, because it meant that even in the middle of a war and with no outside support these people were producing medicines almost to FDA standards. The temptation in the stress of wartime is just to get the product out without worrying so much about the quality. But it turned out the Russians had taught the Eritreans how to do things properly when they were backing them in their struggle. However, Fred's story put me on the wrong track because I imagined an infrastructure much more robust than the one I found when I got there.

Fred had a tendency to say whatever he thought he needed to get the results he wanted. I've seen him with patients and he was the classic gruff, kindly old physician with them. And there was no one smarter than he was when it came to community medicine. Everybody else, though, only got to see the foul-mouthed tough guy. He loved to challenge people: 'Jeez you're ugly, you've got a face like a hatful of arseholes,' was a standard greeting. But he was also a supreme example of how one person can inspire many people to do great things.

His main focus was intraocular lens technology and no wonder. This is such a simple, and has become such a cheap, operation, yet it produces the most spectacular results. Blind people can be made to see again in minutes.

It was developed towards the end of World War II by an English ophthalmologist called Harold Ridley. He was dealing with a lot of fighter pilots who had bits of Perspex embedded in the vitreous or white of their eyes when the plastic canopies of their Spitfires exploded.

He came up with the idea of inserting replacement lenses inside a little bag. They were a marginal success, because when people jumped up and down they ruptured the bag and it got dislocated, but they were the start of intraocular lens technology, which has come a long way since.

Everyone who lives long enough will get cataracts eventually. In some countries it is worse — there may be a genetic predisposition but environmental factors, especially exposure to UV rays, exacerbate it. That means taxi drivers or agricultural workers and people in the developing world in general are more susceptible.

In 1992 the World Health Organization's recommended surgery for this type of cataract operation was to take out the lens and discard it. That meant patients were left with no focusing mechanism. They were then issued ridiculous-looking glasses with huge lenses which were barely effective.

Fred said that was raping people's eyes, and he was absolutely right. In the west, surgery involving a small incision in the eye and the insertion of an artificial intraocular lens to replace the natural one was now standard. The WHO didn't believe that could be made to work in the developing world and kept taking out people's own lenses. Fred was determined to end that.

As far as the lab in Eritrea went, he was clear he wanted me to build it and nothing more. But first he insisted on driving me to Wollongong to meet his South African tool-maker. Driving with Fred was almost as much of an adventure as going to Eritrea.

As we headed down the main highway we encountered silent roundabouts — bumps in the middle of the road, meant to be avoided — but Fred went straight over them in his four-wheel drive.

I didn't say anything when he went over the first one. Then he went over another one. With a big cancerous growth on his back and the drugs he was on, I thought maybe he was just being a little absent-minded and it might be best to say something before we rolled over.

'I think you're supposed to go round these things, Fred.'

'What are they going to do to me, Ray? I'm fucking dying.'

I survived the ride and the meeting. I also realised that the lenses this guy was making weren't up with the latest in lens technology and design. They used what is called three-piece technology, which is flawed because if they go in at a slightly wrong angle then the lens stays twisted in the eye.

I never got a chance to talk to Fred properly about the fact that this was on the wrong track before he died. In fact, I only knew him for five months in total.

Gabi called me not long after the Wollongong trip.

'Fred's not going to make it for another week, if you want to see him. And he wants to meet with you, anyway.'

Everyone went to say goodbye to Fred, ushered into his room one at a time. He was propped up with tubes everywhere. Even if I hadn't been told how bad he was, I would have known because his whisky was a very small one. I was reminded of the med school experiment on T and B cells and alcohol and thought how little it mattered to someone who was in the process of dying.

He didn't waste time getting to the point. He wanted to make sure I wasn't going to back out of my promise once he had gone.

'I'm happy to go off to Eritrea and have a look as I said.' I was hedging.

'Do something fucking useful with your life. Don't make money out of sick people, you bastard.'

I was trying to make jokes and lighten the mood, but he wasn't interested.

'I want you to get those fucking things made. Fucking promise you'll make those?' I felt a bit compromised because of what I knew, but I agreed.

'All right, Fred, I'll do it.'

I did want to make the most of speaking to someone who was about to die. I thought there might be some lesson worth learning from this horrible process, and I asked Fred if he had any regrets.

'I regret not speaking out when I should have done,' he said. 'I should have spoken out about eye care and stuff like that years before I did.'

'Is that all?'

Then the tears came.

'I regret that I won't see the twins grow up.' Ruth and Rosa were only a few years old.

And then I took off to Vietnam to check on a project that I was building there, and flew from there to Eritrea. Fred died while I was away.

ERITREA IS 2000 METRES above sea level. It's a beautiful clean environment and most of the time — day or night — it's a nice warm 25 degrees. But at that time it was getting over its decades-long war with Ethiopia, which had ended just months before. It was the biggest mechanical war since World War II with huge amounts of artillery involved and many deaths — 4000 people in one day. The infrastructure had taken a terrible hammering.

The plane was due to get into the capital, Asmara, around one in the morning but as we approached there was a thick mist — which they often get at that altitude — and we were turned around and dumped in Addis Ababa, the capital of Ethiopia. Then, and probably now, the airport is just awful but I reverted, rolled up my clothes to make a nice pillow and went to sleep as though I was roughing it on the streets.

In cases like this, where I don't really have any control over what is going to happen, I click into the survival mode I developed in Finsbury Park. When you've been whacked enough you don't even flinch any more. Eritrea was good in that it probably got rid of the last vestiges of flinching.

Eventually I was put back on a plane to Asmara and we landed safely. It was night-time again by then, too late to contact anyone at the Ministry of Health to tell them I had arrived. The airport staff wanted me to stay there until the morning, but I had had enough of waiting in airports.

'No, no,' I said. 'I need to go to my hotel.'

I managed to talk my way out of there but by now it was one in the morning and there wasn't a soul around. Asmara is not a big African city — there are only about 600,000 people — so there was no line of cabs waiting for passengers.

I started to walk down the road towards the centre of town and came across what must have been the only taxi at work at that hour. It didn't look good, though — the driver was parked with the hood up, fiddling with the motor. It was a little Fiat 500, which is what the country's taxi fleet consisted of, and none of them was less than forty years old.

'Can you take me to the hotel?' I asked the driver.

'Not going.'

I whipped off the distributor and checked there was a spark. There wasn't.

'You haven't got any spark. Is your battery flat?'

'No, the battery's fine.'

I played around with the battery terminals and gave it a bang, and suddenly the car started. It was my first good deed in Africa.

'I need to go to the Nyala Hotel,' I said.

The driver threw my suitcase onto the roof. And I mean threw

— the car didn't have a roof rack, just a hollow dent from all the suitcases that he had tossed there over the years.

The main road into Asmara is a beautiful straight road with palm trees either side. It is nothing like you expect Africa to be because there are lots of beautiful Italianate buildings, many in art deco style. Asmara used to be called the Rome of Africa. The Italians had occupied the country for about fifty years, until 1941, and left all sorts of traces behind. Much of the city was laid out and the buildings designed by one architect, so there was a harmonious look to the place.

During the war of independence the city was never occupied, although the airport was frequently attacked. However, all the buildings had suffered from neglect, planks were falling off them, the footpaths were a shambles. Big bits of plaster had crumbled away, leaving huge scars on the exteriors of buildings.

When we got to the hotel it was in darkness. The driver and I banged on the door and eventually the night manager shuffled up. I was struck by his plastic sandals, which I later learnt were the trademark footwear of the Eritrean Liberation Front Fighters. To complete the picture, he was wearing army fatigues, a t-shirt, a big anorak in the 25-degree heat, and carrying a hurricane lamp.

He led me into reception.

'Do I need to sign in?'

There was more shuffling and he finally found the book. Then some more shuffling and he couldn't find a pen.

'No. Sign tomorrow.'

He led me upstairs to my room. They were trying to do up the stairs, so all the tiles had been removed and stacked along the side, although work seemed to have come to a stop at that point.

I was taken to what I found out later was one of only three

functioning rooms in the hotel. As furniture had worn out or got broken in various rooms they had contracted until now there was only enough to furnish these three.

By the light of his paraffin lamp, the manager showed me the bathroom, which was a beautiful Italianate space, with a bidet, toilet, shower, bath and two hand basins. It was absolutely stunning, full of marble and brass. Then he took me into the large room which had a double bed, a sitting area and a huge wardrobe.

'Thank you,' said the manager, and he left, shutting the door behind him and plunging the room into total darkness.

That was one thing I hadn't prepared for. First things first. I groped around to see if there was any toilet paper, which there wasn't. More than anything I needed light, so I did a quick mental inventory of my luggage and remembered that I had an alarm clock which had an LED display on it.

Holding that up, I was able to make out shapes of things in the dark and get around the room. I turned on the tap and all I got was a gasp of air. I thought it might have been too high for the water pressure and tried the tap on the bath, but it merely responded with the same asthmatic gasp.

For my first week there, all I managed to get out of the plumbing in my room was gasps and wheezes.

I developed a routine. Every morning I went to the manager's office and knocked on his door.

'My good man, there's no water in my room.'

'Water is coming.'

And water did come, on a truck, about five days later. It filled the tank for a few days and then the cycle was repeated.

I stayed in many Eritrean hotels over the years and they were always an adventure. I invariably asked first if my room had a bathroom. If it didn't you were in trouble, because that meant every man and his dog was shitting into something down the end of the corridor. And they don't just shit into the hole in the ground; the shit gets everywhere, and it's awful.

I once stayed at the Red Sea Hotel in Asmara. The manager there was the by now familiar character who looked like a third-generation copy of Humphrey Bogart in *The African Queen*, with a ripped t-shirt that had sweat stains on it.

I was travelling with Ian Hickling, my mate from Douglas Pharmaceuticals days. I wanted to check everything was okay before I committed to staying here.

'Have you got a room?'

'Yeah.'

'Have you got a bathroom in the room?'

'Yeah.'

It was looking good.

'Can we have two rooms next to each other?'

'Yeah,' he said. 'You have to pay me now and I'll take you up to the room.' That should have made me suspicious, but I handed over the money. And it was only when we went up to the room and he opened the door that we discovered there was no roof.

So that was how I learnt that, as well as asking if my room had a toilet, I also needed to ask if it had a roof.

For Ian and me that was one of the longest nights of our lives, because the mosquito attacks were relentless. We had to cover ourselves in our blankets when the temperature was already over forty.

This manager also had an original idea of what was meant by 'next to each other'. I was in room forty-six, and Ian was definitely in room forty-seven, but when you went along the corridor, once you got past room forty-six, the building ran out.

It had been partially destroyed by bombing and number forty-seven was now on the other side of the street.

SURVIVAL WHEN YOU'RE TRAVELLING in the developing world, then and now, comes down to a few basics. One is attitude — be prepared for the bus to break down, the showers not to have curtains so the toilet roll gets soaked if you're lucky enough to have one, and for the fact that you can't make things happen when you want them to happen. Also, take wet wipes everywhere.

The lack of resources in the hospitality industry extended to restaurants as well as hotels. There was only one menu and every restaurant had it. It didn't matter where you went, you were presented not just with the same options for your meal but with the exact same menu you saw everywhere else. It had been produced for one hotel and everyone else got hold of it, whited out the original name and put their own in. The spelling mistakes were faithfully carried over from menu to menu — like fesh for fish. Grilled fesh was the most common breakfast choice. If you were used to cereal or traditional breakfast food, it was too bad — there wasn't any.

It was only natural, really — after thirty years of war, tourism had taken a bit of a dive and their efforts had been projected into winning the struggle rather than catering for foreigners' appetites. Their main food was lentil soup (which featured on the menu, of course). That is a good sustaining food and I quite liked it, but I had so much of it I swore I would never eat it again after I left Eritrea. It could have been lobster bisque and I would have felt the same.

The cutlery was also a random assortment of items from hotels all over the city, much of it appropriated after the hotels had closed down. But the waiters were so beautifully turned out. In their white shirts and black waistcoats, they could have been working at restaurants in Italy.

And all the hotels had magnificent big Italian coffee-making machines. Unfortunately, they had all broken down and no one had had the wherewithal to repair them. To this day I don't know why I didn't have a go at fixing one, because I reckon I could have. I was busy doing other things, and coffee was not really that important. Partly you got used to things not working — that seemed to be the natural order — so the alternative of fixing them didn't occur to you.

A lot of the hotel culture was about maintaining appearances. Bars were well stocked with spirits — whisky, gin, vodka. But all the bottles were empty. They were put up for display.

There was beer but the bottles had no labels because no one had got around to producing any. You just knew it was beer from the shape of the bottle. The only other drink you could be sure of finding was Zibib, an appalling kick-you-in-the-guts, anise-based concoction. I couldn't drink it. I also discovered that Ethiopian wine is the only wine in the world I can't drink.

Any hardships I experienced in Eritrea were minor compared to what the Eritreans had endured, and my difficulties were more than made up for by being around the people themselves. They are amazingly resourceful and clever people — a little like New Zealanders in their readiness to give anything a go.

Typical of their character was an eye surgeon Fred had become friends with called Desbele Ghebregerghis, Des for short, who fought in the war and had become an all-round surgeon through dealing with things as they came up at the front.

'Where did you learn your surgical skills?' I asked him once.

'By practice,' he said. 'Because, you know, I tried this and if it didn't work I'd try that.' If you had to pick a country in which to have an accident at the side of the road, then Eritrea would be perfect, because everyone knows triage. Everybody knows how to stop bleeding and save lives.

They are mainly of the Coptic Christian faith, which seems to lie behind a lot of their culture. There was no personal animosity towards the Ethiopians for what they had put them through.

They respected them. 'They didn't want to fight. It was just the big guys at the top were making them,' was their attitude.

Their country was screwed up in terms of anything like acceptable healthcare. Instead, the people looked after each other. They loved each other and were very family-orientated.

I was often the only white person on the street. I've been to most of Africa, and in the likes of Nairobi and Kenya, when you walk down the streets, people stare at you because you're whitey white, and you don't know if it is just because you look different or because you're affluent and they want to mug you.

But walking down the street in Eritrea was like walking down a street in Italy. People just carry on with their business. It's all very European. They kiss each other when they meet. And they have adopted the Mediterranean custom of the *passeggiata*, the leisurely evening walk up and down the main street with family and friends, stopping to talk to people along the way or have a coffee before you say good night.

I always encountered several Eritrean women in slacks and jumpers, beautifully turned out and looking like black Sophia Lorens. The Eritrean women are beautiful and elegant and many are the result of liaisons between locals and Italians.

Their traditional greeting is a kiss on each cheek, which the men also did until recently when someone might have given them a homophobic reaction to it. Now they use a special greeting which involves touching the right shoulder of the guy three times. You do it first with a certain pressure, then with another pressure and then the third pressure is higher. It's an art everyone acquires if they stay there long enough.

The one thing that's not great is the standard of driving, which is abysmal. There was only one set of traffic lights, right in the centre of town. These were fixed up and everyone got the message that when the light turned red you had to stop. The trouble was that they stopped when it turned red whether they were at the lights or 200 metres away. That took some educating before everyone got the idea.

Des had a 1966 Cadillac, which was a bizarre thing to see in the middle of Eritrea. Once, he took me up to what was called the Chinese Restaurant, at the top of a big straight hill. The car was gutless and had not been serviced since 1966. Halfway up, it started to stall. Des couldn't work out how to change gear. In the process of trying to find one, he was looking down at the gears and the car started to go backwards.

'Brake, Des, brake.'

'I have a gear here somewhere,' he said, looking down at the gear lever.

I saw houses going by — swish swish swish — until we got to the foot of the hill and rolled out into the main drag. It was a miracle we didn't hit anything.

MOST OF MY DRIVING was done by the taxi driver I met on my first night, who made sure he was always around when I needed a ride. Whenever I came to town he was there. He was the centre of a wonderful moment that summed up the Eritrean spirit for me.

When new, the Fiat Topolino he owned had snail-like acceleration and a maximum speed of 50mph, but forty years of neglect had taken its toll so all he could manage was a maximum speed of about 30mph with his foot to the floor. Once when we were driving down the main boulevard, a long straight stretch of road, a man in a wheelchair was coming down a steep side road to our right. Because of landmines the country had a very high number of veterans in wheelchairs. The Red Cross supplied them with ski poles with rubber tips to help them propel themselves.

This guy turned into the boulevard neck and neck with us. He and my driver made eye contact and it was all on. The guy in the wheelchair went like the clappers, poles flying like pistons. My driver gunned his car which tried to please but just made the most terrible noise and after a while the wheelchair racer pulled ahead of us and threw his arms in the air in a giant victory salute. You would have thought he had won gold in the Olympics. My guy just thought it was hilarious. He couldn't stop laughing.

But it demonstrated that even though this man was partially paralysed there is no freezing the human spirit. That was the force we needed to tap into to get the factory built. If we gave these people a chance they would rise to it.

On top of all their other misfortunes these people had one of the world's worst rates of cataract blindness. Whatever else he did, Fred had chosen the right place to start his lens-making factory.

But the early days were disheartening, as it became clear just what little I had to work with, no matter how enthusiastic individuals were.

I soon found out that the cement works had been bombed so there was no cement, which is pretty fundamental to any building project. Our main builder had only one eye, which was certainly appropriate, given the nature of the job.

Everywhere I looked something was wrong. The wheelbarrow was not a real wheelbarrow — it had been put together out of sheet metal. The spades had been knocked up out of old Toyota car doors. While I could admire the spirit and ingenuity, I couldn't be confident about the quality of the work.

Everything was hard. Everyone was poor. No one knew much about building. I had to teach them basic construction. After all, the past few years had been spent blowing things up, not putting them up.

As those early days went by, the picture got worse. I ran all over town trying to find basic items, but, for instance, there were no electrical cables. There was no vinyl, which we needed for our flooring to make it Good Manufacturing Practice (GMP)-compliant. There was no paint that was any use. And when I did find some paint, the only rollers available were useless things that looked like a Scottie dog with a broom shoved up its arse.

Someone was needed to maintain the lathes that would make the lenses, but there were no electricians who were even remotely qualified.

I went to the local electronics centre where everyone got their things done. It consisted in total of two men and a couple of TVs they were repairing.

That was the last straw. I decided it just was not going to be possible to build the kind of facility we were planning in this country. It was like trying to make a sports car out of bicycle parts. I felt terrible. I had promised Fred, but there was no doubt in my mind the factory could not be built.

I went to the post office, which was the only place you could be sure of making an international phone call, to ring Gabi Hollows and tell her it wasn't going to happen. At that stage I thought maybe we could start again in Nepal, which had been the next country on Fred's list.

Naturally there was a long queue to use the phone, but the

Eritreans are so friendly and amenable they pushed me to the front, where all the sick and infirm people who couldn't stand up for long were.

I was standing behind a woman who was holding a baby wrapped in a shawl. The baby started to cry and the woman unwrapped the shawl to tend to him. And when she did I saw that one side of his face had been burnt away by napalm — the eye was gone to the bone and his shoulder was horribly disfigured.

I had seen a lot of people with bad war injuries, including terrible scars on their faces, in the few days I had been there, but I had never seen anything like that.

I just turned on my heel and went back to the hotel and into the bar.

'Give me a big shot of whisky,' I said, pointing to the bottles behind the bar.

'I am sorry, there is nothing in those bottles.'

Of course. But back in the room I had a bottle of duty-free Chivas I had brought in with me. I drank about half of it very quickly and lay back on the bed waiting for the morning to come.

While I waited, I looked over some material for the plant Kaizen was doing in Vietnam. I was reading by the light of my little alarm clock LED.

'Damn,' I suddenly thought. 'You haven't come very far from sleeping under a railway bridge. You're now in this godforsaken place on a rock-hard bed. There's no useful plumbing. You're still bathing and washing your crap out with bottled water.'

But then it dawned on me. 'Well, I've survived all this before. If anyone can cope in this environment I can.' Moreover I was probably the only person on the planet who had the precise combination of skills and experience to build a state-of-the-art medical device manufacturing facility in a country emerging from a thirty-year war. More importantly, the little guy with the burnt face and Eritrea as a country needed someone to give them a chance at a better life.

Everything that had befallen me, it seemed, was focused in that one moment. Its purpose had been to steel me for this, and for the first time in my life everything made sense.

Next morning I went down to the post office when it opened and phoned Gabi and said, 'You know, look, it's going to be bloody near impossible, but I promise you I will build the lens laboratory in Eritrea. We'll make it work, I promise.'

NINE

Band of brothers

Building the plant in Eritrea was like eating the biggest elephant of all. Conditions were so hard, war broke out again in the middle of it, we had no materials, the skill base was non-existent. After thirty years of war a whole generation was lost. Only the very young and the very old were left.

I was supervising the construction of a state-of-the-art plant to manufacture intraocular lenses to the highest international standards, and even nails were in short supply. The first nails I bought came wrapped up in newspaper, like they would from a hardware store in an English village.

I asked for more and was told I couldn't have any for two days.

'Why?'

'The nail machine is very slow.'

'What do you mean nail machine? Where is it?'

They took me to the nail supplier's house, and in his back garden he had an old-fashioned machine for making them. He put wire in it, then pulled a handle over so that a spring released a head like a hammer's that snapped the end of the piece of wire into a nail head. The other end was chopped off and there was your nail. It was effectively handmade. He managed to turn out about twenty an hour.

We also could not find a circular saw to cut up our framing. Eventually we located a table saw that belonged to a guy who had brought it in from Germany. But he refused to let it off his property so we had to take everything over there to saw it.

There was sporadic electricity, but no cable for wiring. Early on I went to an electronics shop that looked promising. It had a big bright light outside that stood out like a beacon, and inside was a shiny Perspex cabinet with lots of brochures on it.

'Do you have any electronic cable, the sort you'd use for wiring houses?' I asked. The shop owner produced a whole reel of exactly the cable I needed. I was ecstatic. We were going to be able to do this thing.

'That's fantastic. I want ten of them.'

'No, this is the only one.'

'Well, can you get any more?'

'No, sorry. I don't have any foreign exchange to pay for it.'

'Right, is there any other cable?'

'Yes, we have lots of cable.'

He took me out the back where he had scavenged various bits of wire from bombed buildings. But he had just joined it altogether any old how. Green, black, red — he didn't worry about the colours. Cable was cable. Wire it together and put tape around it. It made the wiring in the factory quite exciting, but eventually we managed to put together a working system.

Having just come from Vietnam, where we were building a super high-tech plant and had six architects to design it, I had to keep readjusting my expectations. The contrast seemed to emphasise how basic our working conditions were at every turn.

I didn't have plans of our building till I got there. When I did get them they had been drawn by hand.

'I need to get photocopies of these,' I told the architect.

'We can't make photocopies, but I can draw them,' he said.

That was no good. It would take forever. I went looking for a plan printer and found one with an ancient Gestetner plan printing machine. It looked like it was on its last legs but just might be able to make the copies I needed. But when the copies came back, I could hardly see them they were so faint.

'I need them to be like this,' I explained to the man in the print shop. 'Like mine.'

'Yeah, okay, come back tomorrow.'

I came back the following day.

'Not ready.'

I went back the next afternoon, and it was great. Everything was there and it was all clear.

'I need about six of those so I can give them to the different contractors,' I explained.

His eyes widened in absolute terror. It turned out he and his daughter had sat up all night drawing the lines in by hand onto the faint photocopy.

I MIGHT HAVE BEEN lacking in hardware and materials, but I couldn't have asked for a better team of people to rise to the challenge. They were there to make a difference to people's lives, but their lives were changed too.

Ian Hickling, who had been with me at Douglas, came and stayed for a few years as factory manager, leading the crew that put it all together. He ended up writing a lot of the standard operating procedures and training the technicians.

If anyone deserves the credit for getting the factory up and running it is Ian. He did the hard work in Asmara for month after month while I went back and forth engaged on other projects. It was clear to me that it was taking an emotional toll on him. Every time I came back into the country he had a different hairstyle or colour. When he asked me to bring him a kilo of sodium hydroxide, I assumed it was for another hair-dyeing experiment.

It turned out he wanted it to put down the hand basin in his US$8 a night hotel room to unblock the sink. He used the basin when he needed to go to the toilet in the middle of the night rather than take a long walk in the dark to the communal hotel toilet and as a result it needed a thorough chemical clean-out.

Back in New Zealand, Ian had been very popular with women. Suddenly he was in Eritrea with no decent food or wine, rotten diarrhoea and no premarital sex. Part of me thought that was divine retribution. Eventually he developed a relationship with a beautiful Eritrean woman called Aida, which involved a lot of sitting on a hilltop holding hands and staring wistfully out over the Red Sea. It was a far cry from partying days back in Auckland, but eventually they fell in love and got married.

I think only Kiwis had the versatility needed to come up with solutions to the difficulties we faced. If you had commissioned a team of builders from a construction company to do this job they would have collapsed at the first hurdle because they wouldn't have been able to follow their own SOPs. We made new ones up as we went along.

Phil Smith, who put in our air-conditioning and state-of-the-art air purification system, had nothing to work with. He had to use parts he hunted down in the local metal works, recycled from old machinery and unidentifiable bits and pieces that the owner had collected from the street.

You could also get metal from the tank graveyard. This was an extraordinary sight that seemed to go on forever. It was an area of about four square kilometres, where ruined or obsolete tanks from thirty years of fighting had been assembled. They ended up piling tanks on top of each other because they were running out of room. Once when I went there I saw a man extracting the explosive from bombs to recycle for some other use.

Our flooring was laid by someone known only as Vinyl — we actually forgot his name. He spent most of his time stoned out of his brain on the solvents he used. In his down time he made do with whisky.

Steven Murphy was a jack of all trades, a bit of a rogue and a dead ringer for Rasputin. He did missionary work on the side, taking his guitar downtown and singing Christian songs in the street. It was already a Christian country, so he didn't have to work hard to convert people.

There was no night life — there was not enough power to light any — and people went to bed in the evenings. During the daytime, when everyone was focused on their work, it was all good, but the nights were deadly boring. We ended up making a rule that you weren't allowed to go to bed before nine, because otherwise people peeled off as soon as it got dark.

The food was no compensation. When I had been away and came back into the country it was usually through Frankfurt, so I went to the delicatessen and bought lots of sausages and dairy products. And they lasted about two days. There was a big party and the food disappeared.

I wanted to arrange something so that we could have decent food for a bit longer. The local food was extremely bland, so on one trip I brought back the biggest container of spices I could find. There was rosemary and cardamom and bay leaves and we used to try to flavour everything we ate.

After about two weeks of doing this, one of the guys said: 'You know, Mr Ray, thank you for bringing all of the things, but if you put these fantastic, beautiful aromatic spices on shit it still tastes like shit.'

So we ended up making our own entertainment, which can be summed up in one word: alcohol. We drank an enormous amount, solely from boredom. 'Ray Avery is like a jellybean on sticks,' Ian Hickling once said, 'and he struggles with a lifetime fight with whisky which he vows never to win.' We managed to bring in enough Scotch to keep us going. Wine was too bulky.

When we finally opened the plant — with Eritrea's president, Isaias Afewerki, and Gabi Hollows in attendance — we followed up the official ceremony with a private one where the boys presented me with a trophy made out of a pyramid of toilet paper and a whisky bottle on top, because that's what they claimed it had taken to get the job done.

The boys slept in a dormitory — eight or nine of them. I refused to because of my childhood experiences. Even today I can't sleep in a room with a lot of strangers. It was a small room and it probably was combat conditions — between the BO, the farting and the cramped space. They were spending twenty-four hours a day together and there was little sense of privacy.

I knew they had gone mad when they started taking photographs of their turds and pinning them up on the wall. That's what happens when people have to stay up till nine o'clock with nothing to do. But it also meant they functioned incredibly smoothly as a team and they supported each other though the loneliness as well as the diarrhoea.

When Ian's relationship with Aida was developing he often got invited to weddings with her. He got stuck into the mess, which is a local alcoholic drink made from honey. Also it made a hell of a mess of you. Once he came home so trolleyed we knew he would fall out of bed so we strapped him in. Somehow, during the night he managed to turn right round so his head and feet ended up at opposite ends from the way we had left him, but he was still under the straps. He stayed sick for a long time after that but the other boys looked after him.

The kind of camaraderie that we had is experienced by very few people. It wasn't the sort that develops in war when people are threatened with death every day, but it was similar in that we were cut off from our normal environments and family and friends. There was just us there for each other in this stressful environment, trying to do a big job in a short time.

That's how the notion of the band of brothers arose, quoting from Shakespeare's *Henry V*:

> *We few, we happy few, we band of brothers;*
> *For he to-day that sheds his blood with me*
> *Shall be my brother;*
> *And gentlemen in England now a-bed*
> *Shall think themselves accursed they were not here,*
> *And hold their manhoods cheap whiles any speaks*
> *That fought with us upon this day.*

And we supported each other like brothers should. Most of us went on together to build the next plant in Nepal.

We are all proud of what we did and the little miracles we pulled off to keep it going. If something didn't work we couldn't leave it and come back next week. We had to come up with a solution then and there.

Certainly, for me, it was the closest to joy and to having a real family I ever experienced before I met my wife and had my daughter. I had made these guys my substitute family. They were the culmination of all the families I had tried to create along the way — Wye College, the med school, Douglas Pharmaceuticals. I wasn't looking for love any more because I had enough love. I had the love of all these people and the people we were trying to help. The people I mentored were like my children, and I was proud of them as they set off on their own, like many of the Douglas crew, who ended up heading other pharmaceutical companies around the world.

I ENJOYED TEACHING THE YOUNG Eritreans skills too, because I identified with them and the bad start life had given them. I was doing a Wye College on them, not only educating them about how to make lenses but about the world at large, different cultures and how to be successful and diligent and honest.

As for the team veterans, we're always prepared to jump on a plane and go to the next job because it's the nearest thing to adventure we have experienced. One of them, our microbiologist Brendan Lincoln, rang me recently. He had just got divorced and invited me to dinner because he wanted to have that sense of belonging that he could get by talking to me and downloading. Now he phones up and says, 'When's the next battle?' He will come to Nepal with me to work on a new project. That's great — it means we have an experienced microbiologist who is prepared to function in difficult circumstances and put up with the inevitable diarrhoea and patiently teach people in a language that's not their language.

Ironically, if you get diarrhoea in a developing country, they've probably got a drug combination that's better than anything you can buy at home because they are used to having to fix it. I carry a medical kit with me when I travel and I usually end up giving it to someone else, because I'm careful about what I eat. But once I ran out and went to the local pharmacist because I had a dose of something.

'You want to fix or you want to stop?' he asked me.

'Preferably both.'

'Take this,' he said and showed me a tablet the size of a fifty-cent piece.

'How many of these do I take?'

'Just one.'

Normally you take something every few hours for two to three days, but I took this thing and I didn't shit for a month. That experience also demonstrates that people in developing countries are innovative and can determine their own lives — they just need a leg up and some help with their knowledge base.

SOMETIMES IN ERITREA I THOUGHT I had come up with a foolproof way of making sure something went right — only to be defeated by the human ability always to choose the one wrong option from thirty right ones.

We had a water purification system that was put onto the wall. It had about twenty parts to it, so I made a template of all the holes that needed to be drilled for the various components. We sent that off and it said on the other side 'THIS SIDE TO THE WALL'. When we got there and tried to put it in, it was the wrong way around.

'What didn't you understand about that?' I asked the guy who drilled the holes.

'It said this side to the wall, so I stayed this side to the wall.'

You couldn't blame the locals for how things were. They had more important priorities, like getting a reliable water supply. President Afewerki was trying to galvanise the country. They had terrible foreign exchange problems which presented difficulties for us getting gear in. Then fighting started again while we were there and all the international aid organisations piled out of town. We stayed on. To be fair, the aid organisations probably ordered their people out, whereas we were our own bosses.

My only hesitation was that we had a young team and I didn't want to put them at risk.

'Everybody is bailing out,' I told them. 'We have three choices. We can either try to get out by land into the Sudan, the opposite way to where the fighting is, or we can get on the junket with all the other people and go to the airport and wait for the next plane, or we can carry on.'

They wanted to know what I was going to do.

'I am going to carry on because who knows how long this shit is going to continue? The last war went on for thirty years. My definition of whether it's safe or not is if the airport is still operating and commercial planes are coming in, which they are.'

There was lots of military activity going on, both on the roads and in the air. It was almost safer to stay, however, because the Eritreans had an automatic system for shooting down planes approaching the airport which they switched on when there were no commercial flights due. Anything else was just blown out of the sky.

'That's another reason for not leaving right now,' I said. 'Because if somebody forgets to flick the switch we are all over.'

So they all decided to stay too.

I HADN'T BEEN IMPRESSED by my first close-up look at big aid organisations. And I'm still not impressed today. I have seen them do too much harm with badly planned interventions, and act with too little respect for the people they are supposed to be helping.

One of the rules for our team was that we got close to the locals. If they were going to trust us and take over the running of the plant, which was designed to be a social enterprise that would provide export income for the country, then we had to understand their culture and how they thought.

One example of Eritrean culture that made a deep impression on me became apparent when I was trying to track down a woman who was working for us and rang her home.

'Oh, my child is not here,' her father said. And it struck me that he didn't say 'my daughter' about this adult in the off-hand sort of way we westerners would, but 'my child'. That parent–child relationship was different from the one we are familiar with. To the Eritreans, the family connection is forever regarded as sacred.

'We've got to try not to pollute their society with our stuff,' I told our team. I think we did a pretty good job of that. And as far as getting close to the locals went, three of our engineers married Eritrean women.

But others behaved very differently. The Fred Hollows Foundation had provided a management consultant to help with training the staff. He was a veteran of one of the big international management companies, and he was struggling with the conditions in Eritrea. He stayed in a different hotel because he couldn't hack it where we were staying.

We had language classes so our people could write the SOPs in English to have them examined by auditors from the UK. But it was taking too long for our management consultant and he snapped and said, 'Right, as of twelve today, everybody speaks English.' Which was very counterproductive. They were terrified. You could see it in their eyes. I took him outside and had a few words to him. Then I went back in and said, 'He's changed his mind.'

Most of the foreign aid workers stuck together, and the Eritreans didn't particularly like it. There was an Italian restaurant that had just managed to reopen when things were starting to get up and running again. I went in to get a meal one evening and it was packed with UN troops. UN people had also reserved several tables by putting their bags with the UN logos on them. There was nowhere for me to sit, so I turned around to walk out.

'No, no, Mr Ray,' the manager called after me. 'Come back.' And he took one of the UN bags off a table for six and made me sit down. Before I could do anything he had put a drink in front of me. And then the restaurant started to fill up and finally the people who obviously had been going to sit at my table arrived and they were haranguing the manager.

'Can you get my pizza to take away and I'll just bail out?' I told the waiter.

'No, no, no,' said the maître d' and he went over to the wine rack, pulled a bottle of wine out, opened it and put it in front of me. 'You are an honorary Eritrean fighter,' he said loudly, 'a son of Eritrea.'

Over a few years I saw the unintended unfortunate consequences of aid going wrong — when the United Nations peacekeeping force and other major aid organisations came to town, things started to deteriorate.

This was a conservative society with no premarital sex. Girls who slipped up were cast out of their families and often reduced to prostitution. Yet the girls were also friendly and loved to meet foreigners and talk to them about what the rest of the world was like. Inevitably this led to seductions. Then a five-star hotel was built, which was a very attractive place to encourage girls back to. It also gave the aid workers somewhere to stay at $US350 a night so they were even further removed from the real life of the country. Their excuse was that they needed to be near the airport but I think they needed to be near the bars and swimming pool. I went there on weekends for a drink but eventually gave up because I couldn't stand seeing the foreigners trying to get off with the local girls.

When President Afewerki threw out the peacekeeping troops, people thought it was because he wanted to have independence and control over his country's borders and the front, but I think, knowing the Eritreans, it probably had more to do with wanting to protect his country's young women.

To outsiders, the Eritreans had several qualities that made them appear either innocent or naïve. They were very tactile people. Often at lectures I noticed girls who worked for us casually put their arms around the man next to them. It didn't make any difference if it was an Eritrean or one of our team. It was purely innocent, but you wouldn't find it happening in New Zealand.

Mind you, some of our guys were no slouches when it came to naïvety. There was a local brothel called the Florida Bar which was one of the first places we found where you could get alcohol. The president and his ministers used to meet there if they wanted to have a beer while they talked. They were accommodated in a back room and a guard with a sub-machine gun stayed out the front to keep an eye on things.

I took Phil Smith, who was very religious, there for a beer once. We were talking to girls who were wearing jumpers and slacks, without a skerrick of flesh showing, and who also had their hands on Phil's lap. He thought it was just that standard Eritrean tactile way of behaving. We sat and talked to the girls for a couple of hours until nine o'clock came around then headed back to the factory.

'Did you have a good time?' I asked him as we were leaving. 'Did you enjoy that?'

'Yeah.'

'Did you know that was a brothel?'

'No.'

RECOVERY FROM THE WAR manifested itself in many ways. It was inspiring when you saw two men recognise each other across a street. They might not have seen each other for a decade, separated by the war, and they ran together and hugged, each so pleased that the other was alive.

There was huge respect for other people at every level of society. I never saw any stoushes in bars or aggression between the people. The Eritreans are among the most dignified, trustworthy and inspiring people I have had the pleasure of working with.

The ongoing war with Ethiopia could still get in your way. Once when I had been working sixteen-hour days for several weeks on the trot, Isaias insisted I have a day off. He had been one of the people who made pharmaceuticals up in the caves during the war and became the obvious choice to run our factory.

Isaias wanted to drive me to Massawa on the Red Sea. I wasn't over keen. His driving was unexplainable. Once he drove out of the factory and straight into a Vespa scooter which had been standing out of everyone's way outside the school on the other side of the road. He crushed it into a wall and destroyed it.

The owner came out, and in typical Eritrean fashion, the first thing he did was shake hands with Isaias. Then they looked at the debris of the broken scooter and had a debate about whether or not it could be repaired. They did not know each other, but the problem with the bike was not as important as having respect for each other.

I let Isaias talk me into going with him to the coast, and we managed the drive without mishap. The location had been completely bombed in the war. It was meant to be a beach outing but it was so hot — around 43 degrees — and the water in the Red Sea is so salty it's not really a fun place to go. This is where the Eritreans launched their counter-attack on the Ethiopian forces. Occasionally if you walk just a little off the main tracks you find human skulls from combat that took place years before. Also, there is still the odd minefield.

Isaias and I had been walking along for some time when he suddenly stopped.

'Oh I'm terribly sorry, Mr Ray,' he said. 'Inadvertently I appear to have led you into a minefield.'

From a scientific point of view I didn't find the qualifications 'inadvertently' and 'appear to' very reassuring.

'Don't worry,' said Isaias. 'I've been in lots of minefields,' which wasn't very reassuring either. It meant that statistically our chances of survival were getting worse.

'Don't worry, Mr Ray. God has great plans for you. I will get us out.'

Isaias was as good as his word, but it was a genuinely dangerous situation. A lot of the injuries I saw had been caused by mines. There was a whole range of them because, having lasted for thirty years, the war had left behind, littered around the country, a physical history of weaponry as it had changed over that time.

Because of the difficult terrain a lot of the combat was fought using machines controlled from remote locations. But there was a battle front and Isaias also wanted to show me this one day.

The last thing I wanted to do was see a whole lot of blokes shooting each other, and possibly me.

'Don't worry,' said Isaias. 'There's not firing every day. They just fire sometimes.'

'I'm not really that interested,' I said.

'You should come. You need to understand our country.'

So out of respect I got into his vehicle and we drove for about half a day to the front. We made our way through a series of little trenches to stone walls that were built up with rubble. They were well put together so they could withstand machine-gun fire or even a hand grenade, though probably not artillery fire.

'Do you want to see the Ethiopian front line?' said one of our group. 'I am going to take this rock out of this hole and then you can have a look, but you don't have to have a look straight away because if you look straight away somebody may fire, because they will see the light coming from behind and you may get shot, so you have to just wait a second then look very quickly.'

'No, no, that's not necessary,' I assured him. Knowing my luck I would get the only dyslexic sniper in the Ethiopian army.

Ironically, although he survived the war, about four years ago Isaias had appendicitis, went to hospital, got complications and died. At least he got to see the lab going and he did a great job of managing it and ensuring the ongoing training and quality.

At Massawa I did see huge bombs. They were three metres long, half buried in the ground. There were big craters and unexploded bombs. The debris of war was indeed everywhere, but nowhere more so than in the faces of the people, because of what they had suffered and are still suffering because of the mines.

The cruelty of mines is that they are designed not to kill but to maim. If you injure one soldier you also disable the two others who will be taken out of action while they get him back from the front line.

Modern plastic mines take your own bone fragments and drive them up through the leg like shrapnel, which makes it very difficult to repair. A soldier's leg will be taken out to the knee, but if a girl out herding goats steps on a mine, her leg will likely be blown away up to the groin, which is an horrific injury. I've never seen as many people without legs as you did on an average day in Eritrea.

All these people were called fighters, and they were revered as such because they gave their limbs, and lives, in some cases. There was not one house you went to where a family member had not been lost to the war.

So while we toiled away building our factory, the entire population was trying to rebuild their country. There was compulsory military service still, and those called up were put to work building roads and bridges. They did it with a lot of smarts — if you drove down the main highway into the bowels of the country there was a new 100m-wide trench of a road that had been cleared and would be a motorway eventually. On either side, palm trees were being planted and you saw an Eritrean who might be in her seventies, coming down a green slope carrying a bucket of water and tending to a palm tree. Everybody was doing something.

MY ROLE AT THE PLANT meant I was coming and going in and out of the country a lot, and I developed an SOP for getting through

Customs. It was important to be able to do that without paying big amounts of duty.

To get to Eritrea I had to fly from Frankfurt and through Addis Ababa, where I had to stay either overnight or at least seven or eight hours. I took medicines and equipment through there, usually about five trolleys of it. I had no one to help me, so I had to move one trolley and then go back to get the next one. Adding to my problems was that airport staff in Addis Ababa invented imaginary duties to go straight in their pockets.

I was an easy target for these guys. They looked at me like I was a money pit.

'Okay, that's US$12,000.' They really weren't angling for $12,000, but they thought if they started at $12,000 then they might get $1000 over the counter.

They tried to tell me it was a legitimate duty and I insisted on seeing the relevant statute, which of course they could not produce. Eventually I could outwait them, but it took up a lot of time I didn't have.

I worked on this procedure I call the Ray Avery Magic Wave, whereby every time I arrived I found the man who seemed to be in charge. It wasn't hard — he usually had a cap and epaulettes or gold braid on his shoulders. 'Hello, my name is Ray Avery, I'm with the Fred Hollows Foundation and I'm transporting these drugs to your friends in Eritrea. We're also looking to help you guys but I just want to get these drugs through without any hassles.'

English was his second or third language and I spoke so fast that he had no idea what I was talking about. Then I touched him on the shoulder and shook his hand and thanked him very much before taking my bags to the Customs counter.

'That's US$12,000.'

'No, no, no, your mate over there says it's okay,' I said and waved to the boss with the gold braid who waved back because he thought I was saying goodbye. The Customs officer thought that meant he had to let me through. Then I rushed out before anyone had time to stop me.

The guys used to give me lists of things they needed, so I often ended up with strange assortments of items in my luggage.

The hardest time I ever got was when I had a magnehelic pressure gauge, which looks like a big timing mechanism, some temperature-sensing circuits, which just looked like cables, wires, a little black box and about twenty tubes of silicone sealant that I had taped together to stop them rolling around.

I didn't give it any thought, and threw everything in my suitcase with my clothes on top. But when they put this through the scanner at the airport it looked like the biggest mother of a bomb you'd ever seen.

So, they threw me up against a wall and there was some discussion.

'I can open it and show you,' I said finally, but they weren't up for that. They took me and my suitcase in a truck to the bottom of the airport, with a young bloke who was obviously dispensable as far as they were concerned. He held a gun on me and backed away about fifteen metres and got me to open the bag. Then I had to pull all the bits out and separate them.

'This is not explosives, this is silicone sealant,' I said, and I took the end off one of the tubes and ate it. That seemed to pacify him.

The other strategy I used to slip stuff through was my Somerset Maugham impersonation — based on my schoolday lessons in how wearing the right gear automatically kept you out of lots of trouble. In my white suit and white hat I strolled through the airport like I was the consul general.

On one occasion, a young guy I hadn't seen before leapt out with this small Uzi, which was very shiny and of which he was obviously very proud.

'Stop!' he ordered.

'No, no, no, I don't do this,' I said, and I pushed him out of the way and walked a couple of paces on. Then I stopped and turned around to see if he was pointing the thing at me and I was going to get blown away. He turned to look at the head guy with the braided shoulder pads as if to ask, 'Shall I shoot him?' The guy responded by making circular motions with his hand at the side of his head, indicating I was crazy.

WE EVENTUALLY FINISHED the construction of the building to international standards, and the team from Australia arrived to set up the manufacturing equipment. I watched with dismay as the first lenses were produced. It was painfully clear that the lathe and most of the equipment Fred had bought were not capable of producing usable lenses.

This was another test of character, because I had done what I promised Fred and could have simply moved on, letting the Fred Hollows Foundation sort out the mess. But by this stage the Eritreans had put their trust in me, so I sourced some generic lens-making equipment and started to put in place a plan to make world-class lenses at a fraction of the price of those distributed by multinational companies.

I started to do research on a revolutionary, totally automated lens-manufacturing process, and one day over a quiet drink I mentioned this to the foundation's director.

'How much money would you need?'

'Well, I'd probably make four lathes and, you know, to get all the intellectual property and stuff around it . . . probably about seven to ten mil Australian.'

We left the pub and I didn't think any more about it, but about six weeks later he rang me up and said, 'I've got your money.'

The reason the amount was so high was that this was going to be a completely new way of manufacturing lenses, with different lathe-cutting and milling processes and a whole lot of quality assurance aspects. There was a huge amount of validation time, because we had to work to international ISO 9001 and Conformité Européenne (CE)-Mark Standards. I wanted the Eritreans to be able to sell their lenses around the world so that they could make decent money out of this. I didn't just want to produce lenses for eye camps in the villages. That meant the lenses had to meet international standards or no one would buy them.

We ate up most of that money, but in a country where not so long before the nails were being produced by a man with a little machine in his backyard, we ended up with what we called the FH2000, which was an automated lathe that could make lenses twenty-four hours a day with somebody loading blanks. We invented a 'vacuum chuck', which eliminated the inherent inaccuracies with existing lens lathe technologies. It also reduced the number of reject lenses and the overall labour required.

It was important to me that the lenses we made were of equal or better quality than those from the multinational lens manufacturers. So I sent samples of our lenses for independent evaluation to the world expert on intraocular lens manufacture, Professor David Apple at the Medical University of South Carolina Storm Eye Institute.

'You have chosen a design which we think is an absolute state of the art in terms of surface finish and general Scanning Electron Microscope (SEM) appearance,' he said in his report.

'I've never seen better lens manufacture.'

We had succeeded in doing something that was theoretically impossible: manufacturing world-class intraocular lenses in one of the poorest, most technically compromised countries in the world.

The other result of the new process was that the price of generic lenses plummeted globally. Ours cost three dollars to make, a fraction of what they had been produced for previously. We could get them onto the market for less than ten dollars, making quality cataract surgery accessible to the poorest of the poor.

This was also a perfect example of 100 per cent technology transfer to the local people. I don't have to do anything at those labs and haven't since 2003. We did the job, got in and got out, and they are expanding their operations and product ranges themselves.

Now the lenses are exported to about eighty countries and, by 2020, thirty million people will have had their sight restored due to this innovative lens-manufacturing technology.

TOGETHER WITH DOCTORS from the Fred Hollows Foundation, I wrote a training manual of SOPs for doing modern cataract surgery that was geared towards training more ophthalmic surgeons. I was not renowned for my gross anatomy knowledge and certainly not for anything to do with the eye, but I liked being educated by the surgeons, and I became a bit of a pain sitting in on all the operations and asking so many questions. There's no substitute for observation in any kind of discipline.

They started out practising on pigs' eyes, then worked up to people. It's a relatively simple operation and doesn't need a lot of facilities or equipment. The old lens pops out like a shirt button when surgically removed. When the artificial one goes in, you can see into the eye. It is a miracle operation because it's only a local anaesthetic and an injection to momentarily stop the optic nerve from functioning.

Once the blocking agent has worn off, which is probably only about three hours later, they could have the bandages removed and see straight away. Usually they leave it for twenty-four hours, just for the incision to heal. Then the bandages are taken off, and they can see like a two-year-old. They often see better than they have ever seen. There are stories about people when they get their eyesight back, seeing their daughter or son for the first time. The child runs to them and they close their eyes — which is a very brave thing to do when you've just opened them and been able to see — to feel the shape of the child's head, just to make sure. They have only met them in the dark world before and they know them by touch.

It is not always that profound. Once we were doing a clinic and there was a seventy-year-old farmer who had not seen his wife for thirty-five years. They did the surgery and his wife was there.

'You haven't seen your wife for thirty-five years,' he was asked. 'How does she look?'

'Older,' he replied.

There are very clever surgeons like Dr Sanduk Ruit who can do the operation in about five minutes, which means they can do a hundred or so in a session. People are supposed to wait till one eye is completely recovered before getting the second done, but they often just get up and go to the back of the queue and try to get the other lens replaced.

After we had been doing our work for several years, the World Health Organization finally changed their policy and said the recommended remedy for cataract blindness was lens implantation. So, starting with Fred's initial ideas and passion and through what we demonstrated we could do in Eritrea, we really did change the world.

Fred didn't see that the equipment he started out with was no good, and he also didn't live to see that the whole idea worked, and that we could build the labs. He pulled it off in the end, because he had the original idea. Without galvanising a whole lot of people it wouldn't have come off, and this is why Fred was a true leader and one of the crazy ones who have made a difference in history by having an idea far outside what anyone else was thinking at the time.

A lot of people get put off doing this sort of work in developing countries because they think there will be so many rules and regulations making it difficult. But in practice, I think if you just go ahead and do it professionally and in a commercial way, it will be okay. It is when you start looking for special deals and, often, if you try to work with the local government, which will necessarily have its own agenda, that you get into trouble.

Eritrea showed me that you shouldn't accept crap, so-called third-world technology, ever in any kind of discipline. It showed me we could do these interventions, we could make quality healthcare accessible to the poorest of the poor, and for me this has become my life's work.

I had a few more jobs to do for the foundation, but I intended to start looking at what else was killing people that I might be able to do something about. And with everything I have done, I have made it a rule that the technologies I develop are as appropriate for someone in New York as they are for someone in Nepal.

It's funny how I found my nirvana and a total fit for my skills. That came in Eritrea. I knew I had the ability to build a factory and the number-eight wire mentality to be able to make things work, fix the generator or whatever. I had the street smarts to get others to back us and the science and manufacturing skills to make it happen. It was as if the random eclectic skills I had acquired over a life's work had coalesced into this magic moment.

My band of brothers and I had proven we could change the world and we were just getting started.

Ten

The Maoists have taken the chef

Building our next lens-manufacturing plant, in Nepal, was a lot easier, because of all the lessons we had learnt in Eritrea. The country was also in much better shape. Eritrea was almost impossible. Nepal was just difficult. Even though it wasn't a giant western capital city, and the people had no experience of high-tech manufacturing or even training people for something like making intraocular lenses, if you asked for some plastic pipe or some wiring, somebody could usually find it for you.

The need for lenses in Nepal was obvious because again there was a high rate of cataract blindness and those people who suffered from it were also at risk of other problems. In fact, their mortality rate was four times higher than the norm. Many simply walked off the mountains and perished because they couldn't see where they were going. Others were given jobs like cooking which were fine for sighted people but could lead to horrific injuries to blind people when they burnt themselves. That was the only work option for them, because it was seen as a sedentary occupation, when they were unable to go out and work in the fields. Most people worked in the agricultural economy, so if you were blind in Nepal, you knew you were under a death sentence — you just didn't know when the sentence would be carried out.

So it wasn't hard to persuade people to have the operation, although we did use some innovative social marketing strategies. We had an operating theatre with a glass wall and a closed-circuit television looking down on the actual instrument that was doing the procedure, so you could see the surgeon putting the lens in. People paid to watch their granny's eye operation. At the end, everyone would clap and they could see for themselves that granny wasn't blind any more, and then they would persuade their other relatives to have it done.

That said, working in Nepal came with its own challenges. In Eritrea there had been the war with Ethiopia to deal with. In Nepal, there was an ongoing campaign by Maoists to overthrow the monarchy and establish a republic, which flared up from time to time. Usually we were able to work around it, but sometimes it brought our work to a halt and we were confined to our hotel for days.

A favourite technique of the Maoists was the national strike, in which they set up roadblocks and burnt tyres in the streets, putting the city in lockdown. Anyone who was brave enough to try to break the strike by driving would be stopped and their car turned over and burned.

Initially, we tried to keep working during the strikes because we didn't really understand what services there would or wouldn't be. Once we were walking to the factory and saw a Maoist barricade across the road. As we got near, an ambulance drove up to the barrier. The Maoists stopped the vehicle, got everyone out and torched it. It went up in flames and we went home and waited a few days before we went back to the factory.

While the boys were happy for a few days' enforced rest, I am never content doing nothing. During another strike, I got fed up and decided to try to get to the factory. There was a dodgy second-hand motorcycle shop a couple of doors down from our hotel, so I asked the owner if I could hire one of his bikes. He said no, because he knew if the Maoists got me they would burn his motorcycle.

'What if I buy the bike off you for cash, then I sell it back to you and if it is all in one piece you can charge me twice your normal hire price?'

We had a deal and I struck out for the factory. I have been riding motorcycles for more than forty years and while I may not be the world's best motorcyclist, I am probably one of the most experienced at falling off them. I can lay down a motorcycle on an icy road and surf along quite nicely as bits break off both the machine and me.

So when I barrelled around a corner on my dodgy, Indian-made 500cc lookalike AJS and found the Maoists had a human roadblock across the intersection, I hit the brakes too hard. The bike developed a speed wobble and all the Maoists could see was a Father Christmas lookalike hurtling towards them, wearing a faceful of terror. They parted like the Red Sea and as I passed through the roadblock I offered a brief apologetic wave over my shoulder before trying to regain control of the bike.

I wasn't always as lucky in dealing with the Maoist insurgents.

On one occasion they had decided to disrupt the tourist industry by closing all the restaurants frequented by travellers.

I had arranged to meet with the Australian ambassador at an upmarket restaurant. Because of the strike I phoned ahead to see if they would be open.

'It's Ray Avery — can I get a table tonight?'

'Yes, Mr Ray.'

'I have some very important guests, including the Australian ambassador. Is this going to be okay?'

'Yes, of course.'

'There won't be any difficulty because of the strike?'

'No — just use the side door when you come, because the Maoists are staging a protest outside our hotel.'

So we went. We ordered our meals, had a couple of glasses of wine and enjoyed our entrées. Then there was a very long pause in which nothing happened. Eventually I called the manager over.

'Is there a problem? We've been waiting an awfully long time for our mains.'

'I'm sorry, Mr Ray, the Maoists have taken the chef.'

EVEN WHEN WE WEREN'T being inconvenienced by Maoists, events occasionally conspired against us. Early in my stay, I got up one morning, went to have a wash and grabbed both taps at once to fill the basin. Somehow the plumbing and the wiring had got transposed. I was instantly electrocuted and found myself on the other side of the room. I picked myself up and wobbled down to reception.

'Excuse me, my good man, I've just been electrocuted,' I told the duty manager.

'What room are you in?' was his response.

'302.'

'Oh, there's a problem in that room. But it's not us, it's in the street.'

Less painful but just as frustrating was trying to find a printer cartridge. I found a Hewlett Packard shop in a mall.

'You're the Hewlett Packard agent?'

'Yes, sir.'

'I know that you won't have a cartridge like this,' I said, producing my empty one, 'because it's a very special printer, but you probably have a cartridge-filling capacity.'

'Yes, sir.'

I knew something was wrong with her reaction.

'You haven't got any idea what I'm talking about, have you?'

'Yes, sir,' she said helpfully.

Many of the team from Eritrea signed up for Nepal. The constant developing-world digestive and rectal issues were never far way. Everyone's bowels seemed determined to have their own fifteen minutes of fame. You got used to talking to someone and seeing this strange look of strangled discomfort come over their face. It would stay like that while they tried to resist then suddenly they would excuse themselves and run from the room just in time to avoid a major disaster.

Other mishaps were more serious. The boredom level in Nepal wasn't quite as bad as it had been in Eritrea, but early nights were still standard and we maintained the nine o'clock rule. One evening when we were sitting and waiting for the magic hour, Vinyl broke ranks and said he was going to bed early no matter what.

Our accommodation had been used as the American embassy many years before and subsequently rooms had been added to it from time to time, so it was very higgledy-piggledy. To get to his room, Vinyl had to go up some stairs, walk across the restaurant roof and over a small walkway, less than a metre wide, to what used to be the building next door but was now, in theory, part of this one.

But extending up through the roof was the stovepipe from the fire downstairs, which was what all the tourists used to congregate around in that cold climate. There was a big window there too, that overlooked the garden.

We heard Vinyl go upstairs and get halfway across the planks, at which point, instead of going straight ahead, he turned right — obviously the worse for wear. Equally obviously, he also grabbed this chimney to save himself. We heard him scream as he burnt his hands then saw him pirouette past the window before landing in the garden below.

The rest of us carried on drinking and ignored him.

After a few minutes someone said, 'Do you think he's all right?' and we all leapt up as one and found him half suspended in a bush and perfectly happy.

Fortunately, Nepal did have great food, with a choice of menus as well as a choice of restaurants.

ONE OF THE ORIGINAL BAND of brothers who had migrated to Nepal with us was Steven Murphy, our Rasputin lookalike. He delighted in leaping out of nowhere and scaring the crap out of people. One day, fate got its own back on him. Someone had dropped something on one of the electrical distribution boxes and damaged it. Instead of owning up they had rewired it as a phase to earth. Steven's job for the day was to grind out some lighting brackets using a huge hand-held grinder. He connected the grinder to the faulty box, held his arms above his head and flicked the switch, receiving a massive amount of electricity across his chest. He was flung to the floor where he lay thrashing around helplessly. For a moment no one responded and he could have died because everyone thought he was just playing the fool.

Fortunately someone eventually came to tell me what had happened and I sent for Dr Ruit, the head surgeon at the eye centre. He was not only the head surgeon there, he was the only clinical doctor around. He arrived and lifted Steven's eyelids to look into his eyes.

'He doesn't need a bloody ophthalmological exam,' was my first thought. 'He needs a shot of adrenalin to the heart.'

I didn't really know what he needed, of course. I was just worried.

The doctor eventually began his own version of CPR, which consisted of pushing up and down on Steven's chest.

I was deeply worried by now. There was no change in Steven. He lived at home with his mother and I found myself walking around the room composing a letter to her in my head: 'Dear Mrs Murphy, Your son was a great bloke till we killed him.'

I always had in the back of my mind the fear that we would lose somebody and have to deliver the worst news to their nearest and dearest. I had had enough near misses of my own to know how easy it would be for the worst to happen.

As I watched Steven fail to respond to the doctor's efforts, I kept thinking of all the time in Eritrea, and the things we had survived. He had coped with land mines and air attacks and various bugs — any one of those things could have finished him off. And here, in the relative peace and quiet of Nepal, he had been done for by a stupid mistake with the wiring. After so many near misses, we had finally managed to kill one of our mates.

And just as I was ready to give up, he pushed Dr Ruit's hands away from his chest. 'Get the fuck off me, I can't breathe.'

BEING NATIVES DID NOT exempt the Nepalese from risk. They were as much at the mercy of local conditions as we were. There was a definite feeling that life was more disposable here than in other countries. One day, a local was building a brick wall and carrying a big load of bricks in a hopper. There was a plank that supported him with no difficulty but would break under the weight if he stood on it with his load of bricks. Which is what he did.

He went tumbling down, the load of bricks came down on him, and the rest of the wall he had been working on followed shortly after. This time there was no doubt about it. He had to be dead. No one could survive that. We peeled off all the bricks and found him still alive, but with his head split open, so he got shunted off to hospital in his turn.

But the next day he was back at work, with a huge bandage on his head. The attitude was: life is tough, and you get on with it.

Brendan Lincoln our microbiologist had also come to Nepal after Eritrea. He got terribly sick once and passed out. We managed to get him back to the hotel and call the doctor. He obviously had been poisoned by something very horrible. I had to wait outside the room while the doctor went back and forth. Then I saw an electrician in blue coveralls going into the room.

'They're going to jack him up to the mains and zap him. Like Frankenstein's monster,' I thought.

In fact, he was hooked up to this gear, with patches all over him going to sensors like huge teats. These were very old-fashioned things, and the electrician had been sent out because the doctor didn't have the right adaptor for the hotel's outlets.

Then it turned into farce. Two of the women on our team were sitting on the ground with me, waiting to see if Brendan was going to make it. When I got up and wandered off for a moment, two Indian tourists came up and approached them, because they mistook them for two prostitutes who had been trying to do a deal with me.

Eventually it turned out to be not as bad as it looked. The diagnosis was that Brendan had endotoxin poisoning and a particularly vicious fever.

In the aftermath, and in typical Nepalese style, two locals who worked with Brendan decided to stay with him and keep an eye on him while he got better. They have no sense of decorum or personal privacy, so, for instance, if you are talking to someone and your shirt button is not done up properly, they will reach across and do it up for you.

Because Nepalese people sleep in the same bed at home, this pair slept in the same bed with Brendan, one on either side. This policy was carried right through to other activities, so that if he got up in the middle of the night to have a crap they would follow him and sit on the edge of the bath and carry on a conversation.

The Nepalese are unbelievably hospitable people, which is both very heart-warming but also hard work for someone brought up in the relatively reserved Anglo-Saxon cultures. When you go there, the people you encounter will almost certainly invite you to their house, which is great for an amateur social anthropologist because you get a close-up look at how they live. The downside is that they tell everyone they know that you are coming, and they come along too. The house fills up with people who are there out of respect and friendliness, although all that happens is you end up being stared at by a big crowd — none of whom can speak English — while you eat. They say plenty to each other though and I don't like to think how personal it gets.

AS FAR AS OUR TEAM goes, it's fantastic that if there is a job that needs doing, I know I can call them anywhere in the world and they will drop what they are doing and give it 100 per cent. That is as true now as it was when we were starting out. They give the communities we work in the benefit of their specialities — whether it's electronics, vinyl-laying or microbiology. There is only one thing I know they will never say: 'Sorry, Ray, I can't make it.'

And they come locked and loaded, as though they are heading into battle. They arrive at the airport, bringing the duty-incurring items and the overweight baggage hassles with them. The places we work in are so remote that we might as well be heading into space, so everything has to come at the start. The guys have huge boxes that have been knocked around and battered over the years, but that contain everything we could possibly need, no matter what goes wrong. Except there is always something we do need but don't have. That's when they get really creative and always manage to come up with an alternative.

'I haven't got one of these.'

'Just use one of those.'

'That won't work.'

'It will if you do this.'

'Oh, yeah.'

One of the minor reasons I think these projects appeal is that everyone gets the chance to take the piss out of me. I like to think I can still foot it with them. The competitive spirit doesn't seem to get any weaker with age.

We once had to install some lights in a very big, very heavy concrete pad, using a very big, very heavy concrete-cutting saw. It's a petrol-driven monster that sprays out water while it's cutting through the concrete so it doesn't overheat. It's incredibly tiring to do for more than ten or fifteen minutes at a time.

The guys had been taking turns with it, swapping back and

forth for about an hour when I came along and said I would take a turn. They patted me on the shoulder and smiled like I was some pet geriatric. Which had the effect they probably wanted — I was determined to have a go and prove myself.

Naturally I got the thing and nearly killed myself by going longer and harder than anyone else had. No one seemed to care, or at least they never let on, but leading from the front is high up on the Avery SOP ladder.

We had a big job on our hands. For one thing, the factory was a lot bigger than that in Eritrea. We were very pleased with ourselves when we managed to obtain a huge generator that would be powerful enough to run the whole factory. It was delivered on a huge truck that needed an extra tray welded on to it just to hold this monster.

The problem at our end was how to get it off again because there was no crane strong enough to lift it. The only solution was to get a large number of ropes with which it was tied to various trees and power poles and building parts around the site — together these could take the weight — and then the truck was driven out from under it. So, instead of taking the generator off the top of the truck, they took the truck out from under the generator. Then it was lowered as gently as could be managed, which was not very, onto a lot of big logs over which it was rolled slowly into the building by a biblical team of volunteers and passers-by.

We had an equally perplexing puzzle with some duct work that had been designed and fabricated in New Zealand. Despite everyone's best efforts and planning, when it was ready to install in Nepal there was a big beam in the way, preventing us from getting it where it needed to go. So with a large amount of cursing and frustration the whole job had to be readapted on the spot.

That turned out to be not such a big drama, but then somebody had to get inside this duct, which was only about 250 millimetres high and maybe three or four metres long, and pop-rivet it from inside.

None of our guys would fit, but luckily we were in Nepal not the USA. Even then we had to hunt around to find an extremely thin guy who could squeeze into the space. We oiled him up with axle grease, tied a rope around his ankle so we could pull him out if he fainted or panicked, gave him a quick pop-riveting lesson and sent him in, where he did an excellent job — and lived.

AS WE HAD IN ERITREA, we tried to work as closely alongside the local culture as we could. And likewise I would sometimes see westerners there who just didn't get it. The old triggers were still deep in my head and when I saw someone being bullied it would take me straight back to school days half a world away.

There was a contractor working for us who had designed an air-conditioning system that was being made on site in Nepal. He kept getting things wrong, so the system was failing. But he wouldn't admit that it was his mistake.

Instead he argued with the Nepalese guys, who tended to shrivel up in the face of this sort of aggression. When I heard him calling one a fucking idiot for a mistake he himself had made, I saw red and a bucketful of childhood angst reared up; all the injustices I had experienced became manifest.

'Barry, can I have a word with you?' I said quietly.

I made him follow me around the back, and then suddenly threw him up against the wall and explained exactly what sort of person I thought he was in words of exactly four letters. He had known me only as smiling and jovial Mr Ray, so seeing this other person with wild eyes who was threatening to rearrange his anatomy — and then some — terrified him. He stopped bullying the Nepalese workers and never looked at me quite the same again.

OUR KIWI INGENUITY was being utilised at every turn. In years to come, I would turn my attention from ambitious building projects to ambitious inventions that I believe will change the world. They use the latest technology plus some that hasn't been invented yet. But one of the inventions I am proudest of was made in Nepal, mainly out of ping-pong balls.

We had been getting our water out of an aquifer, which meant it was filtered through rock on its way to us. It was also full of iron when it got here. We had to purify the water to make it medical grade. That requires a very sophisticated plant, which we had, but the iron was just too much for it. We needed to come up with a new way to get rid of the iron before it went into our medical-quality water purification system.

I knew the iron would react with oxygen and then precipitate out, so if we could oxygenate the water — expose it to lots of oxygen — we would be home free.

The locals had a design for purifying water that I called the rocket ship — a big cylinder into which they would pump water and compressed air — but it kept breaking down. What we needed was a large surface area to spread the water over. I came up with the idea of a giant basket full of ping-pong balls, which create a lot of surface area in a relatively small space. If you poured the water in at the top, by the time it got to the bottom it would have been in contact with lots of air. You end up with precipitated iron oxide at the bottom and clean water floating above it.

'Can you get me lots of ping-pong balls?' I asked the head of the laboratory.

'How many do you need?'

'I don't know — probably about two thousand.'

And I think we used all of the ping-pong balls in Nepal, but that thing is still there, and it's a great example of something wonderful that happens every so often in science — it's what we call an increasing efficiency device, which means that the more something is used the better it gets at doing its job. In this case, as the iron oxide gets built up on the surface of the balls it makes an even larger surface area. I love the fact that there is a high-tech plant doing multi-million-dollar work — and out the back is a water purifier made of old ping-pong balls.

THE TECHNOLOGY TRANSFER generally went smoothly in Nepal. One of the things we had to do in order to be able to leave the place self-sufficient was teach the local technicians how to maintain the lathes.

When we designed the lathes, instead of a whole lot of complicated circuit boards with lots of things that could go wrong, ours was broken down into smaller units with little lights, and you could quickly isolate and identify a problem when one came up. These were nicknamed BRTs — Big Round Things — and if there was something wrong, a BRT's light wouldn't be shining and you just replaced that unit.

Our verbal SOP was: 'If the light is not on the BRT, then the BRT is fucked. Replace it.' This became incorporated into the documented maintenance manual but without the vernacular.

Once I happened upon a Sherpa girl who was lying on the ground with the million-dollar lathe in pieces all around her, like the biggest Swiss watch you ever saw.

'Do you know what's wrong?' I asked.

'Yes, sir.'

'Will it be fixed today?'

'Yes, sir.'

'And you know what's wrong? You really know what's wrong?'

'Yes, sir.'

'What's wrong?'

'BRT fucked.'

I realised we had made more of a cultural input than we had intended.

WE OVER-ENGINEERED the factory so that it would be beyond reproach when it came to quality assessments and audits conducted by international regulatory agencies. By the end we had written out some 400 standard operating procedures concerning aspects of the plant, for everything from how to take care of your raw materials to how to put a label on a bottle. Many of the SOPs were quite short but others were twenty or thirty pages long.

Hilary Holloway, our document controller, was a giant at making this happen. She was a lover of mine for a time during my early days in New Zealand, before becoming a full-time friend and frequent collaborator. As a passionate scientist, she worked huddled over a kerosene heater for hundreds of hours, but it all paid off when we received international accreditation for the factories.

We enjoyed training local people. The Nepalese have always had a tradition of moving to other countries to live. Many of our protégés now work overseas, but they trained people to take their place before they left because we taught them that was what you had to do when you had been given a skill. You passed it on. And as they move around the world, the general level of skills will rise as they take knowledge with them.

One of the reasons they can travel with their skills is that we designed the factories to be better than any others in the world — because if there was one chink in the armour, the multinationals who were our competitors would find it and exploit it to their advantage.

For instance, lathe-cutting lenses would normally be done in an ambient environment — which means just the normal type of atmosphere you would get in an office. But we wanted to cut down the risk of bio burden — the bacteria and everyday germs that float around people — so we made our environment free from bacterial contamination.

All the research into production efficiencies Phil and I had done at Douglas — brightness of the lights, best temperatures for working at — were transferred over to the plants. The aim — and the result — was to have something that could not and would not be downgraded or described as 'third world'.

WE HAD A GREAT OPENING for the plant, with the king doing the honours — the Maoists must have been having a week off.

I had been in New Zealand just before the opening and brought five chilly bins full of live crayfish to the party. Nepal is one of the few countries in the world where you could bring in live crayfish from overseas and get it through Customs. We went to see the chefs in one of the big hotels and produced our crayfish. They were terrified — they had never seen anything like these giant scorpions in their lives. They weren't going to go near them. So we got a fourty-four-gallon drum, cut it in half and made our own barbecue to cook them on.

Now, everyone's job was done. Everyone is always very staunch when we part, and there is really no need for sadness. The band of brothers never says goodbye because we all know we will see each other and work together again. And when we do see each other we just continue the conversations as though we have never been apart.

After we left, the plant continued to go from strength to strength thanks to the genius who ran it, one Rabindra Shrestha. They moved to another level of commercialisation and now make soft foldable lenses and a range of other medical devices. There is no difference in intelligence between cultures — just a difference in resources. Once you get technology into developing countries, they have the capacity to run with it. It's as important to enable that growth as it is to set up a plant in the first place.

The Nepal factory is owned by a private trust — not the Fred Hollows Foundation — and all profits are reinvested in the business or programmes to benefit local people. That is a good example of ethical business to me, using the profits from medicine to improve people's standards of health.

DURING THE YEARS WORKING to get these plants started I went back to England on behalf of the Fred Hollows Foundation, and this trip was notable for two reasons.

The first was confirmation that I didn't belong in England any more. Every moment I was there I felt more and more like a New Zealander.

When I left in 1973 the coal miners and the train drivers were on strike. On my return I went to catch the tube. There were a few people around. I thought it was the queue for tickets and stood at the end, but I realised after a while no one was moving. I went up to the counter.

'Can I get a ticket, please?' I said.

The man behind the counter pointed to a little sign.

'Can't you read? We're on strike.'

'I left England twenty years ago and you guys were on strike then,' I said. 'Have you been on strike all this time?'

I couldn't go anywhere. I couldn't go to the coast to look around and reminisce, even if I had wanted to.

I ended up stuck in a hotel, one of those English places that only the English can create. A hotel where you can walk down the corridor and you can see all the floorboards going up and down, all warped, and big locks in the door and no windows that open, all screwed shut. There's a heater that's connected up to the hot water that you can't turn off. There's no ventilation and no in-room facilities for tea or coffee. It just reminded me of what I had left behind and why.

I know there is England on a good day with the old houses and the wheat fields and the country lanes, but the good days are very far apart.

The second important thing that happened on that visit was that a couple of days before I left the trains started going again and I managed to see Jack Wise, who had set me on the right path when he got me into his rural horticulture course forty years before.

He was out when I arrived, but his wife welcomed me and let me hang around until he got home. It was my last day and I had only about half an hour to spare by then. There had been a 'local boy makes good' story about the Eritrean plant in the paper, so he knew a little about what I had been doing.

'Have you done any double digging recently?' was his opening. Double digging is a technique for turning soil.

'No, I haven't been getting much dirt on my hands,' I said.

'Don't use that bloody word. It's soil not dirt.'

He said something complimentary about the work in Eritrea and I was glad to be able to tell him that all the credit was ultimately his for rescuing me when he did. Seeing him then, I was struck by the similarities to Fred, a really rough diamond, but a very caring person. He had once told me he had never met anybody that he couldn't love or didn't like, and that included murderers who he met doing his prison visiting. Like Fred, he was a true humanitarian. And like most humanitarians he will probably never be recognised properly. Jack died not long after that visit.

After Nepal, I also decided I had done all I could for the Fred Hollows Foundation and I had a simple plan: I was going to develop products that would change the world and save millions of lives.

ELEVEN

Nobody's as smart as all of us

Having got the lens-manufacturing plants up and running and had time to look around the developing world, I saw that there were more acute healthcare issues that needed addressing. You can't spend long in those countries without getting a sense of things that need to be done.

When you sit around hospital waiting rooms throughout Asia and Africa for hours at a time, waiting to see people and sell them intraocular lenses, you learn a lot about primary healthcare in general.

The script, when I finally got to speak to someone in a position of responsibility, usually went like this: 'Does everybody that you treat get an intraocular lens?'

'Oh, yes, yes, yes.'

But I stayed and watched and realised that probably only 5 per cent of patients got lenses. No one was willing to tell you that, because it made them look bad. So, you had to sit there and get the real answers. From the social anthropology point of view, the time I had to spend waiting was most enlightening.

It inspired me to set up Medicine Mondiale — French for World Medicine — as an international development agency. It used all my natural entrepreneurial skills, my artistic abilities and my scientific analytical training. And it drew heavily on my supply of empathy — perhaps the only good thing I carry around from my childhood. To be a serial entrepreneur one also needs a huge amount of tenacity and sound business sense and I had that too.

I conducted a comprehensive analysis of how effective major development agencies, such as the WHO and UNICEF, our potential competitors, were at making quality healthcare accessible to the poorest of the poor. There was no point setting up an organisation which duplicated the activities of existing agencies. How would we be different? How could we be more effective? What could we offer that other agencies had missed?

Sadly, my research uncovered a litany of well-meaning healthcare interventions that had caused, and continue to cause, preventable deaths in countries that put their trust in many agencies. Poor science is being deployed with fatal consequences. These are described and discussed in detail in the last chapter of this book.

I concluded that there was a need for a development agency that would apply good ethical science to solving endemic healthcare problems in the developing world.

I decided to make Medicine Mondiale different from other aid organisations and not build a huge infrastructure. Instead, it is a virtual organisation. When I was at Douglas, I was running what was effectively a virtual company. We had multi-site manufacturing divisions, and everything was managed with SOPs and lots of telephone calls. So with Medicine Mondiale I did not see the need to set up a bureaucracy with a huge number of employees who would eat up all the funding in overheads. I would ask my mates to help me when I needed help. I would set up a lab in my garage, and reach out to people with the right skill sets and add that to my knowledge of distribution industries and business management skills. And I would change the world.

Every day, I spend several hours dealing with emails to connect one part of the enterprise to another. The Liferaft infant incubator we are producing probably has twenty people across the globe working on it, and they're all working for nothing. I'm just the link for the work, throwing in a few ideas from time to time. My real skill is in acquiring other people's expertise.

Nobody is as clever as all of us. New Zealanders are good at live research — we put two and two together, and I don't mind sharing my two with your two to make five.

The work with the Fred Hollows Foundation — and even the work with Douglas Pharmaceuticals — had taught me that things people never dreamt were possible could be achieved. We had to convince people that the eye operations could be successfully performed by writing procedures to train people, getting that up and running, then getting the lenses out there. We had to make videos to demonstrate to the WHO at its conferences that our process worked so that they finally changed their recommended treatment for cataract blindness.

I also learnt the value of a personalised relationship. I wasn't in it for the money or the glory, but for someone without a family it was rewarding beyond description to have a stranger come up to you and thank you because they could see again.

As well as developing quality products which are affordable

and improve healthcare for the world's poor, Medicine Mondiale has a second function that is carried on alongside the first, though it is much less visible: to monitor and evaluate independently the quality and effectiveness of global healthcare initiatives sponsored by the major aid organisations.

UNLIKE MANY OTHER ORGANISATIONS, when we devise our products we take the anthropological point of view and watch people to see what they really need. A lot of inventors start at the other end and say, 'How can we find some technology and make something sexy, and how can we sell it to somebody?' That doesn't get you an incubator. That gets you an Xbox.

You can make money either way, but I would rather take the way that improves the human condition.

We have three main products in different stages of development: the Acuset device for controlling doses of IV medication; Proteinforte, an easily digestible infant food to combat malnutrition and diarrhoea; and the Liferaft incubator, a much more affordable and effective alternative to what is available.

It's a slow process because everything has to be done to the highest standard. Fortunately I have developed an extraordinary tenacity thanks to my childhood experiences, when I had to believe that things would come right one day, and they did.

Now I'm eating the biggest elephant of them all, but we don't want to fall into the trap that the other aid organisations do, which is getting something out there that's not properly tested. Real interventions that work take a lot of planning, and quality is the major input that you need, to make sure that what you're doing makes any difference at all.

It takes a long time to do that testing because there is so much of it. For instance, we're working with a company in

New Zealand to do the software management of the computer control system for our incubator. We have to prove it will work in a whole range of negative situations: Does it work at low temperature? At high temperature? If you put too much voltage through it? Would it wear out over a period of time? The worst-case scenario is almost certain to happen, so you have to be prepared for it.

And even in the field of aid, marketing is essential — you have to educate people about the product and why they should buy into it. Hopefully, because the price is going to be so attractive, and because it's so well designed that it meets all the end-user requirements and they love using it, there will be no obstacles to deployment.

Another principle of the Medicine Mondiale approach that has been carried over from the lens work is 'McDonaldising' our products. Basically: do you want fries with that?

The lenses came in two kinds — the extremely cheap developing world version that could be put in at eye camps where thousands of patients went through in a day, and the more expensive foldable version for sale to the high-end customers.

With our incubator, for instance, there will be a basic version that will be super cheap, but there will also be a more expensive version with a microprocessor connected to a computer that records data about the baby and sends them to a remote nursing station. The same Proteinforte will be sold very cheaply for babies at risk, and at an extremely high price to endurance athletes for whom it is a super food.

Science should be sexy, and we make our products sexy to give them broad appeal. They should feel good in the hand and look as good as they function. The lenses in their cases were streamlined like a Ferrari. And the incubator we are creating will look like the spaceship that was used to fly baby Superman to Earth from Krypton.

All this is possible because of my experience in applied science, which has been behind everything I have done, from fiddling with radios and TVs as a kid to setting up plants in Eritrea and Nepal.

A good definition of applied science is taking everything that is known currently and applying it to a new paradigm. Another useful definition was given in the TV show *Blackadder* when one character had written a book and another accused him of plagiarism because he had just rearranged words that were already in the dictionary. Science is the same, a matter of rearranging fundamental bits of information.

I asked my friend Colin Murdoch, a great New Zealander, and inventor of the disposable plastic syringe which has saved millions of lives around the world by preventing cross-infections, what makes a good scientist, and he said, 'Someone who sees the world differently.'

And he's right, because we are all looking at the same world, but some people can see it very differently from others. Some people take a piece of wire and bend it, and it's just a bent piece of wire. But if you heat it up and bend it, it becomes a paperclip or a hair grip.

A scientist called Percy Spencer was working with a magnetron as part of research into long-distance radar detection for submarines in World War II when he noticed that a chocolate bar in his pocket was melting. Eventually, he came up with the idea of a microwave to heat food.

More money would speed our work up. We genuinely do most things for nothing and I subsidise the shortfall. I pay for the phone and the stamps, but there are no offices except my home, no plant except the lab in my garage.

It is a magnificent facility, a true scientist's lab the equal of anything in a hospital or university and it was given to me by Novalab, the country's leading lab builders. I asked them for it, and they gave it to me. I am determined that you don't have to have a lot of money to make a difference, a principle that goes hand in hand with the belief that poor countries can produce first-rate equipment without big budgets.

However, if somebody gave us $10 million then the incubator-development time would probably come down from three years to eighteen months because we could go out and buy some things we need instead of waiting for them to be donated to us. Ultimately we will not be able to avoid spending about $2 million to get it properly certified and approved internationally.

At the same time, I don't want to be in the position of employing a bunch of project managers simply because I can afford to. It's more efficient just using people as you need them. Somebody does the design of the case, somebody does the design of the sterilising system. It's empowering for them to work for nothing and the people that are involved feel they have really done something.

People don't care about being paid if they know they are making a difference. It had never occurred to Vinyl that he could make the world a better place by laying flooring. But he has, as have patent attorneys and the microbiologist and everyone else who works for free. The patent attorneys have given us tens of thousands, if not hundreds of thousands, of dollars' worth of pro bono hours. Eventually the Liferaft will be fully patented. The primary patent is filed but there is more to do and we will get that done for free too.

One of my greatest assets in this work is that the small amount of charm that I once used to get bread rolls and cake for free can now be used to get a few more dollars when I need them or professional services for nothing. I'm constantly humbled by how far extremely busy people will put themselves out for Medicine Mondiale.

A BONUS FROM BEING named New Zealander of the Year in 2010 was that I got asked to speak to numerous groups, which meant I got to meet a lot of people who could be — and were — of great value to Medicine Mondiale. For instance, I spoke to some foodstuff suppliers, and by talking to them I can steer them to be part of our distribution.

I'm not just a scientist. I'm a commercial animal and the commercial model is right for this kind of aid work because it's about creating, marketing and distributing a product in an economically viable fashion. It's not about caring for people with your great big heart. Just like the magnetron, we could look forward to some profitable unintended consequences from our research that could put money back into our work. The air-purifying technology being developed for the incubator could be used to purify the air in your car or your home.

The band of brothers has proved themselves with Medicine Mondiale. When it was time to start work on the plant in Nepal where we are going to produce Proteinforte, I rang the old team up, and, as I knew they would, they all agreed to come. But there was one big difference between working for the Fred Hollows Foundation and working for Medicine Mondiale.

'You're going to have to spend your own money to get there,' I said, 'because Medicine Mondiale has none.'

'We're in. Best holiday we can have.'

These people inspire me, as do the few real humanitarians I have met in my life. One was a man I was introduced to in

Australia. He was wearing a cheap Timex watch, an ordinary pair of slacks. It turned out he didn't own a car and he always flies economy. His name was Chuck Feeney and I had never heard of him.

'What do you do, Chuck?' I asked.

'I used to own some gift shops,' he said.

Later, someone told me he was the founder of DFS, the world's biggest duty-free store chain which he had sold to Louis Vuitton for billions. He has kept a few million for himself and is giving the rest away. That's how he spends his time.

I have ongoing business interests but all my money goes to Medicine Mondiale. I live in a middle-class suburb and drive a sixteen-year-old car. I know so much about what a difference money can make. I've lived like a millionaire and I've had to look for cardboard to put in my shoes to cover the holes so I could go out. Now I'm more interested in what I can achieve in the time I have left to me than in what I could spend money on.

ONE OF THE FIRST PRODUCTS we will commercialise is the Acuset, which was the result of seeing how people on drips got their intravenous medicines when I was waiting around those developing world hospitals. IV therapy is the most widely used medical intervention in the world.

I was alarmed to see potent substances such as anaesthetics, chemotherapy drugs and antibiotics being administered using a simple gravity infusion set. In a first-world hospital, such treatments are administered using a highly accurate $2500 electro-mechanical infusion pump. But in the hospitals I visited a simple twenty-cent roller clamp was being used to control the dose, often in the hands of an untrained and incompetent relative, with often fatal consequences. One or two millimetres of movement of the clamp can be the difference between life and death, particularly for a preterm infant on a drip.

We have fixed this problem in our societies, but no one has tried to do anything about it in the developing world. This picture really highlighted for me the fact that science has abandoned a large part of the planet's population.

The conclusion was obvious: if we could make accurate IV drug administration available at virtually no cost, we could save millions of lives. Our Acuset device effectively means you can dial the right dose. It's incredibly simple, incredibly cheap and it still took us three years to get to the point where it can go out to the market. We did every test we could think of, including dropping them from great heights and running over them with a truck, because they need to be close to indestructible. But it's magic — a lifesaver that costs mere cents which anyone can use.

PROTEINFORTE HAS BEEN considerably more complicated, but is another sexy miracle of applied science. It's a high-protein food that very sick infants, who will otherwise die of malnutrition or diarrhoea, can digest. A lot of children suffer from acute protein-energy malnutrition. They don't have enough energy to maintain their essential organs, so they shut down.

We're building a plant to produce Proteinforte in Nepal and will use that as a training ground for building more plants in other countries.

The other aid organisations have been looking for a magic bullet for the problem. They thought it might be vitamin A. It wasn't. They thought breastfeeding was the answer. It didn't make any difference. They came up with a rehydration product where the osmolarity — the concentration of the salt solution — was too strong. That ended up killing children because the kids it was fed to ended up dehydrated and if they weren't put on an IV drip in time they died.

These solutions overlooked root cause factors that couldn't be fixed, like dirty water.

But it's clinically proven that amino acids are important for kids. If they are at death's door, you can keep them alive by putting amino acids into them.

In a first-world hospital the sick children go into an incubator with an IV drip of amino acids going straight into the blood-stream. That gets the mitochondria working so they have some energy. But amino acid therapy is too expensive to be used widely. I needed a cheaper version of that.

I remembered back to the kiwifruit handlers wearing gloves so their fingerprints wouldn't be exfoliated away. We found out how to break down big proteins into amino acids, using kiwifruit enzymes, and put that into a very dilute solution. If you can get that into the kids, the amino acids go straight across the gut and that gives them energy so they can digest the rest of the food that's in the mixture and start to build up some strength.

As well as being cheap, it also had to be palatable. We had to come up with formulas that were near in taste to their natural foods or that could be adapted very simply. In Nepal, the most common dish — at the end of the day, or even for breakfast — is lentil soup and rice. A few vegetables might be added and chicken very occasionally.

Chicken was our solution — high protein and palatable. Globally, billions of tonnes of edible chicken waste is thrown away every year, so there is an almost endless supply of our main raw material. In New Zealand when we were first developing this, Tegel gave me frozen slabs of waste chicken meat the size of a dining table that I had to cut up with a chainsaw. That got quite colourful at times and made the neighbours slightly worried.

In Nepal, we found a chicken processing factory and are building our plant there so it is easy to use what is left over from their production. We also needed a source of enzymes for the amino acids. We expected to have to grow pineapples for that but, to our astonishment, when we got there, across the road from the chicken factory was a pineapple plantation.

We had worked out the right combination of amino acids, peptides and pre-digested protein back in New Zealand. We tried our recipe out on kids in hospitals to see if they would eat it and they loved it.

The next step was to see if it would have any effect on infant mortality. This is a very difficult thing to test. You don't want a trial where half the kids are going to die because they're on a placebo, but at the same time we needed to see if it would have any effect on increased body weight over a period of time.

We began by feeding it to rats and they all put on more weight than rats fed on milk formula, which was encouraging. After that we did a trial with just twenty children. In the end, we discovered that really sick kids suffering from protein-energy malnutrition fed on Proteinforte were four times more likely to survive than those fed on any other sort of food — milk formula, soy formula or breast milk.

We will do more tests when the factory is finished — it makes sense to be testing with the product we are actually going to make and sell.

The enzyme component presents its own challenges, which we are still working on. We need to dehydrate kiwifruit or pineapple to powder so we can transport it around the world. Freeze-drying is a costly process. We found another technique, costing about a tenth of that, which looked very promising, but it created a

Calvin reaction which means the amino acids don't go across the gut so effectively. That's science — often more error than trial.

For now we are stuck with freeze-drying, but there are some other innovative technologies coming along that may give us the alternative we are looking for. At the end of the day good ethical science will prevail.

Nepal has been a great place to try these things out. The people are super adaptable and will try to do anything you ask. Because I'm known from the lens plant, the people at the hotel I stay in have gone the extra mile and provided a rug on the concrete floor in my room and some bigger furniture for me. They even made a mini bar by dragging in a full-size fridge and putting everything in there — from whisky to red wine. And they didn't forget the snacks — there was a sack of peanuts on the floor next to it.

Our third and probably most spectacular initiative is the Liferaft incubator, the sexiest and potentially most miraculous piece of applied science you will possibly encounter.

YOU WILL ALMOST always find two things in the hallways of developing world hospitals — people on stretchers because there is no room for them anywhere else, and broken infant incubators.

With nothing much else to do while I waited, I looked at the incubators. Perhaps they just needed a fuse replaced.

'What's wrong with that incubator?'

'Doesn't go.'

'Can I have a look at it?'

I got my penknife and found the overload switch that just needed to be pushed and the incubator suddenly came back to life. Or I took out the filter and cleaned it and the incubator was good to go again.

My first idea was to get someone to go around fixing the incubators. But it turned out these expensive machines had an average life of about 18 months. Because they are exposed to the ambient environment — which means that traffic fumes and any other nasties in the air get in — the filters get worn out very quickly, then the heater circuit overloads and the machine shuts down. There is no way they can be kept in a sterile environment, so it is impossible to keep the filters clean. It was obvious a specially designed incubator needed to be developed to cope with these conditions.

Even when the incubators were being used they seemed to do more harm than good. There was a disproportionate number of kids in incubators who had pneumonia and upper respiratory tract infections. It seemed odd because the kids in the general ward, who weren't in the incubators, didn't have the same symptoms.

We had access to local microbiological testing labs, so we took swabs and found that the bugs inside the incubator were up to 150,000 times more concentrated than what we would see in an incubator in the developed world. In our hospitals, the incubators get cleaned regularly, the babies get cleaned and their nappies get changed. In developing countries the babies get sick, there are not enough nursing staff, and the sickest children get put in incubators where 95 per cent of the air is re-circulated, complete with bacteria. Worse, humidification units are filled with local tap water, rather than the manufacturers' recommended sterile distilled water, and within hours the levels of pathogenic bacteria become life-threatening.

We needed an incubator that sterilised the air inside the incubator constantly.

And I needed a sterilisation unit that would last for ten years. Typically, sterilisation of air is done with a fluorescent UV light, which is good for about one year. I decided to find out what NASA did because they have craft that are away for a long time and need to have sterile water and air. It turned out they had developed systems for sterilising water and air using LED technology.

I took that information and worked with it, and now our incubators have a little box with a range of LEDs, and when the air passes through, the LEDs sterilise it. Better yet, they are solid-state devices so they don't wear out.

And while we were there, we adapted the fans by slicing a bit off to make them run quietly so the kids can get some sleep. And we re-engineered them to run first one way then the other so the air goes in two directions and the incubator filters become self-cleaning.

There was a lot of number-eight wire technology in the first iteration of the prototype Liferaft incubator. We have done basic things it's hard to believe no one did before. For instance, we have made it easy to clean. The inside part comes out and can be taken to a wash bay and hosed down and sanitised without buggering up the electrics.

Instead of following the proportions of standard incubators, I reversed the process and measured a baby. I asked the design guys to make me a 3D computer image of a six-month-old baby and we worked the dimensions of the incubator out from that. Most incubators are much bigger than they need to be.

It's constructed of polypropylene so is pretty much unbreakable and also lightweight. The organic egg shape is very appealing, especially, I've noticed, to women.

First-world versions have portholes through which you are supposed to be able to change a nappy or a catheter safely. But what happens in reality is that staff just open the incubator up because it's easier. The portholes are a needless expense.

We were determined to design our incubator to world-class standards because one common failing with international aid agencies is that they dumb down technology for use in developing countries, often with life-threatening consequences. For instance, there's an American organisation that built an incubator out of car parts. Their thesis was that if you made it completely out of car parts it would be locally serviceable and cheap because all the spare parts from broken-down cars could be used as a readily available source of spares.

But there are two flaws with that. One is that to heat up the incubator they use car headlights, which are full of mercury and terrible toxic metals, so their naïvety means they might end up killing somebody. Secondly, the notion that there are spare parts lying around the third world is false. Any parts that become spare are immediately grabbed and used to repair existing cars. Anyone who has tried to buy a spare part for their car in these countries knows that no one stocks the part and it's prohibitively expensive. There is an awful lot of bad science deployed in the developing world and those who have put their faith in us for help deserve better.

In contrast, our incubator will be approved by international regulatory agencies, such as the US FDA, so it can be sold to any country in the world. And that takes time and money. Probably 75 per cent of the budget for the Liferaft will end up going to meet regulatory requirements. But it will be worth it.

And now we have a working prototype which people can smell, touch and see. We can use that to attract venture capital, or, hopefully, to get a serious donor with a few million dollars who will really want to make a difference and provide money to commercialise the product. It's a bit like the lathes for producing low-cost lenses — it cost \$7 million to get the first lathes made, but the technology revolutionised lens manufacturing and brought down the cost of lenses globally

I THINK MEDICINE MONDIALE has a huge future. There are young people working with us who can be trusted with it when I am gone. Water quality is probably the biggest single problem in the developing world, and perhaps something will arise from the LED technology to help with that. I can't see any potential magic bullets for other serious problems.

One of our donors visited our projects in Nepal and, having seen the enormous healthcare problems, said, 'I don't think that any money I give will make any difference to changing things in Nepal.' My band of brothers and I take a different view. We are the crazy ones because, as the Apple ad says: 'Those that are crazy enough to believe they can change the world are the ones that do.'

We can't solve all the world's problems, but we know we can save a lot of lives with our products, and maybe some of the children whose lives we save will grow up to find more solutions.

I know more than most that everyone deserves a chance at life.

TWELVE

Woman in a White Dress

In my early fifties, I had long since given up any hope of
marrying or having children. I hadn't been especially moved by
any woman I had met in years. I had been involved with some
who were very special, and all in their own ways paved the way
for me to become a better person. There were one or two I might
have been able to have a proper long-term relationship with, but
I wasn't in the right frame of mind at the right time.

I was focused outwards on trying to fix the world's problems,
and there might have been an element of loneliness in the
motivation for that. There was a part of my life that was not
fulfilled.

My life had alternated between rather placid, gentle academic
environments, like Wye College and the medical school, and

the hard-edged, cut-and-thrust business world. In middle age I craved a peaceful, serene existence, and then love came along, in Nepal, of all places.

It was late 1999, and I was there for a big summit meeting between the Nepalese and the Eritreans about how they were going to divide up the global intraocular lens market, so that they wouldn't be cutting each other's throats commercially.

I was holding forth, giving a lecture to a roomful of people about marketing lenses internationally, when the door opened and the Woman in the White Dress walked in and I fell in love with her. She was the one I had been looking for. I knew that. I knew it instantly. I even knew in that moment what it would feel like to kiss her and I knew that when our lips touched it would be the softest spell and it would penetrate my heart and consume me. That she was obviously at least twenty years younger than me didn't deter me in the slightest.

Her name was Anna Kiousis, and she was an Australian of Greek descent who worked in the aid field. She was there because an economics professor friend of hers had invited her to look around the lens laboratory. While doing so, she discovered the meeting was on and decided to look in.

Anna had been working in international aid for other organisations for several years and had come to the same conclusion as me — she didn't like what she saw many of them doing, so she had set up her own charitable organisation, Barefoot Economy, helping poor people, particularly women, develop sustainable businesses. She even had the same attitude to financing her work. She has only had a selected number of donors and the rest of her funding has been from her own efforts.

Of course, it was all very well falling in love, but I was out of practice. I had no idea what to do, and this time it was important. However, I could tell just from the way she spoke to the Nepalese people that she was a gentle woman with an extraordinarily good heart. But for all I knew she was married with eighteen children. I needed to come to her attention. And although she had wandered in, she wasn't listening to anything I was saying. She was talking quietly to the person next to her.

Then I remembered seeing a programme about Khrushchev talking at the United Nations. He took off his shoe and banged it on his desk to make a point. It worked for him . . . so I took my shoe off and started to hit one of our lens cases to show how strong they were.

Anna glanced at me but didn't notice me. Shortly after the talk I got the chance to show her around the lab. I tried to rev up the presentation but I could tell she just thought I was a nice, smiley-faced, nerdy scientist.

The next day everyone travelled to a hotel called the Fort, nestled at the base of the Himalayas. The weather was glorious. I was sitting behind Anna, watching her beautiful black hair bounce up and down on her shoulders, and I felt really happy for the first time in years.

I still knew nothing about her. I couldn't ask her outright if she was married. If she had been, that would have been the end of it. And I wouldn't have been bereft — it would have just reinforced my impression that she was an extraordinary woman. I almost expected her to be married.

So when we arrived at the hotel I wrote her a note on the back of an SOP about sterility testing and waited for an opportunity to give it to her. The power went off that evening and, just before dinner, I helped Anna to her room with a torch.

'This is for you,' I said, and handed her the note just before she shut the door. Then I ran away.

She thought it was something to do with work, she told me later, because it was so badly presented and given to her so casually. She put it in her pocket and forgot about it while she got ready for dinner. Then she remembered it and started to read it by torchlight.

The Fort
Kathmandu Valley
Nepal
Nov 99

Note from a small island (preface)

I cannot recall when construction of my small island began. The first sandbags of sadness were clearly laid down in the orphanages where I learnt to become self-reliant. But my construction proper of the sea wall to keep the world's storms at bay became concrete the more I travelled in Asia and Africa.

Sad at man's inhumanity and the falsehoods we are forced to work with, I retreated to this small island. This is not a sad thing because I enjoy my own company. And on clear-weather days I take the boat to the mainland where I put on a jester jacket and make people laugh. I move freely amongst people, safe in a cloak of knowledge.

Content within myself I can see the roads of others and have found great freedom in the ability to give absolute love to others.

When I am abroad I never (usually) see myself in the picture. On the island I promise myself that I will start painting again soon. Yet I know this will not happen. Although my greatest passion is to paint, my objective with any painting is to let the audience see the world in a different, more realistic way. And this is the catch 22, because I cannot justify the selfishness of creating a painting that perhaps a handful of people will enjoy when, in the same timeframe, I can contribute to hundreds of people regaining the gift of sight. This has to be the best picture of all. In the past seven years I have been consumed by this endeavour and it has given me great joy. But in some ways I have given up so much of myself that I have become numb.

Until that day when I first saw you. Suddenly, without asking, you filled my world with love and beauty.

These words are for you to thank you for bringing beauty, which I had lost, into my everyday world:

> She comes easily into the room wearing a shy
> smile. Sits in the chair, gentle curves through

Thursday's clothes. He can no longer hear what is being said. She has captured his senses.

When expressions are at rest he can see the peace that she brings him.
When she smiles that smile, and those small creases form around her eyes and her nose when she laughs, she takes his breath away. She is a terrible beauty.

He had forgotten he could feel this way. She arches her back to rub the sore patch at the base of her spine and he feels like a thief in the forest watching a young freckled deer dart flicker flacker amongst the beech forest, stopping to listen to some unseen sound.

He is embarrassed. Wanting to sweep the hair from her face; to trace the lines of her body. He had forgotten passion.

But this a small shard of a broken mirror compared with all the peace she brings him. He does not wish to interfere. He has no life to offer her. He is just thankful and very happy to watch her and be close to her.

When he hugged her goodnight the actor was
still on stage, but just for a second as they parted
there was a magic moment when their fingertips
touched and he knew that far off on the magic
island he would always remember her smile.

You are a very lovely woman.
Thank you for brightening up my world.

Love, Ray x

By the second page she realised it was a love letter and panic set in because she had no idea I had anything like these feelings for her. She didn't know what to do.

We were all downstairs ready for dinner — everyone except Anna. The economics professor she was travelling with called her room and she came down. By sheer fate the only seat at the table was next to me.

During the meal, we talked about everything except the letter, which was fine, because I really needed to learn about who she was.

I found out she was from Sydney. She was not married. Her father had a painting business, and was a charming larrikin who had jumped ship to settle in Australia. She had one brother. The family lived in Maroubra at the centre of a big Greek community and, most importantly, she didn't have a boyfriend.

After dinner she went to bed and I continued dividing up the world between the Eritreans and Nepalese until four in the morning, by which time we had finally hammered out an agreement.

The next day we travelled back down the mountain. I was trapped in the back of the truck between a bunch of Eritreans and Nepalese and Anna was in the front seat. I had devised a plot whereby I was going to meet her at the airport or at her hotel and then take her to lunch somewhere special and talk about things. We still hadn't acknowledged the letter. As we got close to her hotel, there was a traffic jam and Anna's travelling companion was worried about getting to the airport.

'We're going to get out here and walk to the hotel, Anna,' he said.

They got out, but she stopped half in the door of the truck.

'Are we going to see Ray again?' she asked.

'I don't think so,' he said, and he slammed the door and the truck went off.

And when the rest of us got back to the hotel later, we found out the Eritreans had sent all their things to the airport with an arsenal of souvenir knives and swords and lots of food in their carry-on luggage. I had to go to get it all sorted out, so I didn't actually see Anna again. I went off to Vietnam and she went off to Bangladesh.

Three months later I had managed to get a number, and I called her up to say hello. I was trying to impress her so I put on my best RADA accent.

'Hello, it's Ray Avery here,' I said.

Anna was dealing with a major problem in Bangladesh at the time.

'Ravi? Ravi who?' she said.

It took some of the momentum out of my carefully orchestrated call but we ended up speaking non-stop for about three hours.

Later, I invited Anna to come to New Zealand.

THE DIFFERENCE FOR ME between everything that had happened before with personal relationships and this one was that I knew everything was going to be perfect so I had no agenda. When she came, we even had separate beds.

In a way, our relationship was sealed with a version of my old dream of helping the Woman in the White Dress across a stream, except the roles were reversed.

We rode bicycles down to the beach for an outing. I went hurtling ahead, approaching the speed of light, to impress her and make sure she knew that I had what it took, despite the age difference. But I hit a stream which turned out to be twice as deep as I expected and the bike came to a sudden stop. I tried to get off but when I lifted my leg up the whole thing went over. The water was freezing cold and when I stood up my jumper was down to my knees because it was soaked.

'Oh God, I hope she's not worried that I've hurt myself,' I thought.

I looked over and she was lying on the ground, cracking up laughing. I picked myself up and we went for a walk. I like to be dry and clean as a rule, but I remember lying on the beach completely covered in sand and dirt and wet through and being totally happy, and I had my head in Anna's lap and she reached down and kissed me. She took things into her own hands, and then it was all on for one and all. That was a very natural thing. That was everything.

'If you had to pick a moment when you fell in love with me,' I asked Anna once, 'when would it be?'

'When we were driving down to Puka Park Lodge,' she said. 'It was a beautiful summer's day and the roof of the car was down, and you were in your shorts and your t-shirt and you were just driving. I felt this overwhelming love and affection because we were talking about what you do and what I do and all of that.'

She knew who I was. She didn't know the back story about my childhood, but she had seen me in Nepal with people and formulated her own picture.

We kept our relationship going from our respective countries for about eight years. It was a long-distance liaison, which meant we avoided the blah bits that you get when you marry somebody and start doing the washing-up and the laundry together. You get longer to underpin who you are. We haven't given up our identities for the relationship at all. Being together but separate, in the sense we weren't living in the same house, we developed a special kind of rapport and appreciation for each other. And when we were together it was always romantic.

It didn't hurt that when we did meet it tended to be in exotic locations where we were travelling for work. It was a case of 'Can you be in Bangkok in May?' or 'When are you next in Nepal because I can go when you're there?' and it would be nirvana for us.

It can be lonely doing that work, particularly at night, when you've finished what you have to do, and you get back to your hotel room and it's the same food night after night.

We stayed at interesting hotels as well as good hotels. By the nature of our work, sometimes our romantic get-togethers would turn into some duty, such as a hospital visit for someone. But we each accepted that.

There has been a meeting of souls because of what we know about development and what works and what doesn't work. We both think similarly about what's important in life.

We also both understand that in the developing world, shit

happens. You can be sitting at breakfast together in a nice hotel, which is not where you're staying but where you've gone for a nice meal because your own accommodation is budget and dodgy.

So you grab half an hour of paradise, but in the middle of it your girlfriend will say, 'I've got to go,' and you know she's gone to the shitter and she'll be there for some time with a gut-wrenching diarrhoea. Once we met and Anna had just been in India and she had dysentery. I spent that visit filling her up with electrolytes to keep her well.

Luxury wasn't the norm. Most hotels where we stayed had beds with no springs — just mattresses on wood. It's good for your back, but you have to go into rehab when you get home. A lot of women wouldn't be up for it, but Anna has done the same gig for years and she's not a fragile woman. I find it worse doing a Rotary Club talk and having to stay at a cheap chain motel in New Zealand.

If I was travelling through Sydney I would stay to see Anna and I got to know her family well. After a few years her mother finally cracked.

'I'm fed up with this. You two get married,' she commanded. So we did, with a big fat Greek wedding in May 2007. The bride's side of the church was full and the groom managed to scrape up six people for his side.

Anna's family knew that we had something going, and they liked me as well so that made a big difference. I loved them. When I married Anna I got the perfect family. They are filled with love and free of any angst. Her mother is a gorgeous woman and a fantastic cook, and her father is an attractive man. He still walks with a swagger and I think he's got a sense of mischief like I have, which has helped him accept me. He wouldn't have wanted his daughter to end up with a nice accountant.

The age difference never came up, but for some it provided amusement.

There was a wonderful moment in Nepal once, early in our relationship. We were going through Customs and the young official said, with typical Nepalese lack of inhibition, 'Are you two together?'

'Yes,' I said, and he smacked me on the bum and said, 'But she's so much younger than you. Naughty man, naughty man.'

'I'm after her because she's rich,' I told him.

There have been times, especially in the early days, when perhaps you look like a new couple, that we went out and it was obvious that people noticed the disparity. I worried about it for Anna's sake.

'They're not looking at us because I'm old,' I told her. 'They're looking at us because you're so gorgeous and wondering what a gorgeous girl is doing with a git like that.' If it still happens, we don't notice any more.

Initially having a baby had not been part of the plan. We were still spending long periods apart with our respective projects after we were married. And I was averse to being a father anyway because of what my childhood had been like. But when we began talking about it I rationalised it. I knew that on Anna's side our child would always have a big, loving family. I knew he or she would be looked after by these incredible, extraordinary people.

'If you want to have a baby, maybe we should think about it,' I said, about a year after we were married. It was more out of love for her than for the idea of being a father.

So, it became a possibility in theory, and the first time we were in the same country at the same time, and it was possible in reality, Amelia was conceived. We thought we would have many more relatively free years without this responsibility. We had nine months.

NEEDLESS TO SAY, MY YEARS of abuse have had a big influence on how I behave with our daughter, who was born in 2008. It's a life-changing experience, having a child, but probably more for me than most people. It reopened some of that old stuff. It's a reflection of what should have been for me, and that makes me love her more.

I know there are people who keep making the mistakes with their children that their parents made with them, but there is no way Amelia will ever know any violence. I understand how fragile life can be, but I know we have a choice about that, and I choose to make ours joyous.

I want to give her a life that she wants to lead, and make sure she has exposure to everything that is good about this world. There will never be any set of circumstances that I can imagine where she would get a smack.

There's a great piece of Indian spiritual wisdom along the lines of 'Don't associate with evil people because you'll become one' and it's true. If you focus on getting even and finding the perpetrators, you're only hurting yourself. Amelia has helped redeem me. There's not a day that I don't hold on to her and give her a hug. When I hold Amelia, the little boy trapped inside me gets to have the hugs he didn't have years ago. It's like having a second childhood and a second chance at the perfect life. I want her to have the perfect existence that I didn't.

Anna too has redeemed me, but the adult side. Amelia touches that totally visceral stuff that's been locked up for so long.

She has taken over our lives. She's a midget but she's also a truck that rides over and destroys everything. We used to have a nice ordered life with everything polished and clean and just so. Not any more. But every day you see some new bit of enlightenment in her eyes and that gives me great joy and enthusiasm and when she hugs you, you feel that you have found paradise.

My age makes a difference, and again I can relate that to my own childhood and the way the kids from the orphanage were set apart at school because we looked different. We had second-hand clothes and jackets were always too long and shoes were stuffed with paper because they were too big. There was a stigma associated with who we were.

I don't want Amelia to be at school and getting second looks because her dad doesn't fit the norm. That's going to happen because of my age, but I'm sixty-three going on sixteen. Her dad will be taking her to school in a sports car, and he may be an old fool but he will also be slightly dangerous in an exciting way. I'm getting going in life and still finding it exciting and I'm still adventurous and fearless.

I think if there's a sign of the coming of age it's that my petrol-head side has got to the point where instead of having a beautiful blonde getting in and out of the car, I have an even more beautiful brunette sitting beside me in a baby seat.

Also, I know I'm probably not going to see her be married and many other things, so I just cherish the moments we have every day. I don't see that as a bad thing. Some people have long lives with their children that are full of misery.

Anna's got her own development agency so Amelia will be brought up and maybe take over her part of the business or maybe she will be inspired to get involved in some things that Medicine Mondiale has been working on.

Also it gives a sense of excitement, because I watch the little nuances of how she engages with the world and I think it's fabulous. She's like my biggest science project. By the time she is five she will be making her own range of cosmetics. Not because I want her to be like Dad, but I want to give her the opportunity to know stuff.

I have a vision of her being dropped off at school with her little heart-shaped glasses, skipping off into the future. Then she will come home and her dad will take her into the laboratory and show her how to make cosmetics and fragrances or whatever she wants. Or she will fly off to be with her mother in Nepal. I like to think that if I give her the right kind of background and right education, she might change the world as well. She will get the chance.

I'm not sure how much our children inherit from us. I did worry in the sixties and seventies that I might have got my father's uncontrollable philandering gene and would never be able to behave differently. If I'd turned out to be like him I would have been devastated.

Amelia is certainly a good little scientist and I will teach her science from the start. We were watching *Play School* and someone was getting a piece of corrugated cardboard to make a roof, and I found myself saying, 'We can do better than that. That's not practically sound. It wouldn't make it. Look at all that tape they put on there.'

I see bits of me in her even now when she's pouring things into little containers. She's got that single-minded determination that I have. She just goes for it.

Once at the museum she was interested in the rock pool that is under Perspex and she couldn't see it properly because of the reflection from the lights. I watched her realise this and work out how to get into a position where she could see what she wanted. She is only eighteen months old and she is thinking about the world at large. And I will do everything I can to encourage her to explore things and be brave and tenacious.

I hope that, if she gets nothing else out of her time with me, she will feel that anything is possible and she can look back and read this book and say, 'My dad was a good bloke.'

And I want her to have a good heart.

Amelia was not yet born the second time we got married. Because our Nepalese friends couldn't come to the wedding in Sydney, they insisted we go there and have another ceremony. We married at the local temple and it was the first time any Europeans had ever been married there. There were about 300 invited guests but, because there is not a lot to do there, all the people from the surrounding villages turned out as well, so it was quite a crowd. And as we drove up through the mountains to the site, they left their houses with their children and babies and sat on the side of the road, waving as our procession went by.

Friends came from New Zealand and Anna's family was there. It was an extraordinary ceremony which included things like Anna's parents having to wash our feet and yoghurt being flicked at us. I had to be led around by her as a symbol of my duty to look after her. It was full of colour and music and there were beautiful robes and flowers, even if the man performing the ceremony was dressed like a taxi driver. It was a wonderful, humbling experience.

When we got back to our hotel it had been converted for a party and candles had been placed all the way up the stairs and along the passage leading to our room.

Now we both do our own stuff, although our projects are side by side in Nepal. Anna wanted to set up a social enterprise that worked and Barefoot Economy does that by paying farmers an above-market price to provide raw crop materials that are used to make essential oils. The plants are grown in the highest part of the Himalayas. They are absolutely pure and clinically very good oils, produced from a very high-tech distillation facility.

The farmers make money from selling the plants, and then money made from selling the oils is repatriated back into the project so it can grow bigger the next year. The Proteinforte factory and the essential oil manufacturing facility are side by side.

My life is glorious in that all of the things that I was looking for, I've now got. All the things that were missing have been found, not in the discos where I had been looking for love, not in the world of commerce where I had been looking for success.

Every time I look at my wife, I remember how much I love her. Lying in bed with her and with Amelia tucked in beside us is the greatest reward I could have. My hand used to reach out and clutch the hands of strangers who were taking me away to live with them. Amelia's little hand reaches out and is grasped by her father's or mother's hand. Together we are secure and we protect each other. And now we are thriled to find that we are about to be parents for the second time.

That's my paradise. It also makes me think I want to give those kids who are dying because they don't have an incubator a chance at that. They should be able to hold their father's hand and I intend to make sure this happens.

THIRTEEN

Killed in action

At the age of sixty-three, I find myself enjoying all the blessings a man can have. My life is having a happy and, I hope, long ending.

As I have become more deeply involved in aid work I have also become more deeply concerned at many widespread practices which do more harm than good. Medicine Mondiale intends to fix this in two ways — with our own life-saving products and by establishing an Ethical Science Group to monitor global healthcare interventions to make sure that, at least, they do not kill people.

An underlying problem is that most aid agencies need to justify their existence and fall into the trap of thinking that being seen to do something, even if it is not helpful in the long term, is better than appearing to do nothing in the short term.

It's easy to feel that way — children are dying; something must be done. But sometimes, nothing is better than introducing poor-quality initiatives which do not improve healthcare outcomes. There have been too many cases where interventions have harmed people.

It's convenient for organisations to give sick children a little bar of something and say: 'Take this away and eat it,' rather than having them in a clinic where they get better care. So many bad health initiatives are born out of the one word: 'action'.

A further trap is that once a commitment has been made — which is nearly always in the many millions of dollars — it's easier to keep throwing money at the problem rather than cutting the losses and investing time and money in looking for a better solution. Everyone is in too deep to be able to walk away. This insistence on sticking with the discredited remedies diverts money from the potentially effective solutions.

My philosophy is that if you're not actually fixing things, why not wait until you can, rather than wasting money on ineffective programmes that keep donors happy?

IN JANUARY 2010 A report published in the English medical journal *The Lancet* showed that a $27 million UNICEF programme — IMCI, or Integrated Management of Childhood Illness — that combined numerous strategies and was deployed across several African countries for several years had failed. In fact, some kids who were not on the programme had a higher survival rate than kids who were on it.

There's something odd going on. The IMCI programme is not treating the right diseases, or there is some unknown, underlying disease that is killing children, and it's probably to do with primary healthcare and poor water. If you give kids vitamin A, but they get diarrhoea, they're going to die. If you have a successful breastfeeding programme but they get diarrhoea, they're going to die. The focus needs to be on things that are killing the kids and not these side issues.

In 2007 a *Lancet* editorial slammed UNICEF over its self-congratulatory claims that the UN agency had produced a steep fall in child mortality rates with IMCI and that its global healthcare programmes had reduced under-five infant mortality.

The Lancet had sent a copy of a research paper prepared by Chris Murray, Professor of Global Health at the University of Washington, to UNICEF for comment prior to publication.

Murray's paper stated that 'globally we are not doing a better job of reducing infant mortality rates in the developing world than we were thirty years ago'.

Six days after receiving the article and prior to its publication in *The Lancet*, UNICEF called a press conference announcing 'A major public health success'. *The Lancet* concluded that UNICEF was acting contrarily to responsible scientific norms that one would have expected the agency to have upheld. Worse, it risked inadvertently corroding its own long-term credibility.

What is clear to me is that UNICEF 'spin-doctor' any potential adverse publicity, and while we may anticipate dodgy finance houses and investment companies doing this we somehow believe, and want to believe, that UNICEF is the real deal.

The Acuset IV device we are making is a good example of something that addresses an underlying problem that no one had seen. When we looked closely at what was causing deaths, we recognised this hidden factor of people being given too much medication because the delivery mechanism was not precise enough. They weren't dying of those diseases — in many cases, they were dying from the treatment. By making it cheap and easy to give the right doses of medication, we can save millions of lives.

Colin Murdoch's disposable syringe exemplifies this thinking — no one had really thought of how reusing syringes was re-infecting people. Reusable glass syringes were the industry standard, a part of the system so taken for granted that no one thought about them. By making syringes that could be used once only, Colin saved millions of people, and probably saved the western world from an Aids pandemic.

The fault in many cases is sloppy science. Anyone following proper scientific methods would not be having these problems. In the rush to be seen to be doing something, solutions don't get the initial rigorous experimental testing and independent scientific testing they need to ensure they are effective or safe. We wouldn't give things that had not been trialled properly to children in our country. In fact we're really hot on that: 'It's not been proven, don't take it.'

The development agencies have guidelines, but you would not be happy if I said, 'I'm going to do a brain operation on you. I don't have any experience, but I've got some guidelines.' For any intervention, you've got to have a Standard Operating Procedure which shows you how to do things in a proven and consistent way. That's been borne out in Eritrea and Nepal where we have had perhaps a 300 per cent turnover in staff in the lens laboratories over the past sixteen years but lens quality remains as good as ever.

AID EFFORTS CAN GO wrong in any number of ways, at every step along the chain. Complicated exercises such as vaccination programmes are extremely problematic. Vaccines go off like a cut lunch in the sun, losing their activity in as little as eight weeks in ambient temperature. They've got to be kept cold, but getting a cold chain that streams right through the programme in a developing country is near impossible.

People end up not getting the true vaccination, or being given double the dose because somebody miscalculated things, which is what happened in one case where the High Court of Assam in India found UNICEF guilty of causing the death of kids who were administered a toxic dose of vitamin A. UNICEF implemented a blanket vitamin A supplementation campaign in two districts in Assam in 2001. In giving judgment, the Chief Justice said that the health workers involved in the programme were not properly trained and briefed and had administered greater doses than many of the children could tolerate. UNICEF had introduced stronger doses of vitamin A by replacing a traditional 2ml dosing spoon with 5ml medicine cups.

What makes this story more tragic is that a comprehensive scientific survey conducted by the Indian Council for Medical Research in 1999 showed that vitamin A deficiency was not a public health problem in these areas.

UNICEF has a global programme to roll out vitamin A supplementation and clearly it did this in Assam without determining whether it was required. It was simply a waste of money and cost the lives of those who put their trust in their caregivers. They were simply killed in 'action'.

We tend to believe people who have senior positions in respected, high-profile aid organisations, but who have made too many bad judgement calls to be trusted.

Applying commercial standards to aid remedies will not only improve global healthcare outcomes, it will also make sure donor funds are not wasted. For instance, bed nets used to treat malaria cost $30. If, despite all the other problems with them, you get them to people, then under stringent clinical trial conditions they have been proven to save five children for every 1000 bed nets distributed. That's 0.5 per cent effectiveness, which doesn't add up economically when you consider how many provably workable solutions could be funded with the millions of dollars spent each year on bed nets.

Under non-clinical trial conditions, the locals simply tire of hiding under a bed net at night and the result is that bed nets alone are not effective in preventing deaths due to malaria.

In March 2010, Malawi's deputy Minister of Health advised that the country's campaign to fight malaria through the distribution of one million bed nets had failed to curb the number of deaths caused by the disease. That's $30,000,000 wasted donor funds.

At Douglas and when building the lens-manufacturing plants, quality was a key commercial priority. I'm trying to get the word 'quality' injected into international aid programmes. If we can do that, and people start thinking about the quality of the programmes they employ, then we will see improvements in global healthcare and we won't see a huge amount of money getting wasted because of 'action'-driven global healthcare strategies.

AID IS ALREADY A BUSINESS. Organisations compete with each other for funding. I have known senior aid workers to rejoice out loud when a hurricane or tsunami occurs. That's an attention-getting event that they can do a fundraiser around. It will be on television. The money will come in and the overheads will be taken care of for a few more months.

Development agencies have an ongoing political problem because they have to be donor-focused. If people give you money, they want to see you doing something with it. That also drives them to do things and to be seen to be doing something at any cost — even when that cost is people's lives.

Medicine Mondiale does not have that problem because we accept money only for things that can't be given in the form of services, skills or labour. We're not under the hammer to be seen to be performing. People who give us money understand the bigger picture: that you need to invest a lot to get a life-saving medical device into the market, because it's more complex than giving away a few vitamin tablets.

If we invest in social enterprises, or education systems that generate revenue, then we do long-term good. Setting up a polytechnic to teach trades would be a smarter move in the developing countries than giving a lot of people some pencils.

A huge amount of the resources and energy of large aid organisations is also applied to the media and building the edifice of the organisation. There is a lot of self-promotion. To get that you need to have a quick fix so you can show you're doing something and there is something for the cameras to look at.

People won't really want to hear about a complex process and be told, 'We need to put in a whole lot of micro-enterprise details that make it all work.' They want to hear: 'This $10 will buy clean water in a village.'

It's all made easier because in developing countries there is no reference point. At home in New Zealand, life is governed by a set of unwritten rules about how you behave. For outsiders in developing countries there is no reference point.

I know and appreciate that people want to give money to an organisation that seems to be trying to fix things, even when they know about the difficulties. 'We know a lot of it gets burned up in overheads but we've got to try something' is a common attitude. Naturally, it makes people feel better to give, even if they know that much of it may not get to the right people. There's a little bit of redemption in it for every donor. Unfortunately, they are feeding the problem by giving financial support to people who are doing, in some cases, more harm than good. They think this is 'better than doing nothing'. It's much worse, and it's using up resources that could be deployed effectively.

PERHAPS THE WORST EXAMPLE of what I am talking about is the litany of mistakes that were made in Bangladesh following a cholera outbreak in the early 1970s. In trying to fix this problem, UNICEF made all the errors outlined above and ended up responsible for what has been described as the biggest mass poisoning in history.

The aid organisation spent millions of dollars over many years drilling a million or more backyard tube wells in an effort to provide clean water for the population. The wells used subterranean water sources as an alternative to surface rivers and ponds, which are prone to bacteriological contamination. The thesis was that if you drilled deep enough you got past all the bacteria that are common in ponds.

If they had planned better, had some basic quality standards, SOPs and adopted WHO guidelines for water testing, they would have found that the water from more than half of these wells they sank was tainted with carcinogenic arsenic. Today, more than thirty years later, more than twenty million people are still drinking water from tube wells containing life-threatening concentrations of arsenic.

By 1993, the general population was showing telltale signs of chronic arsenic poisoning, including skin lesions, cancer of the skin, bladder, kidney and lungs, and neurological and pulmonary diseases.

Four years later, in 1997, despite evidence that the arsenic-contaminated tube wells were causing a major pandemic, UNICEF stated in its 'in country' report for Bangladesh that it had surpassed its goal of providing 80 per cent of the population with access to 'safe' drinking water in the form of tube wells, ring wells and taps by 2000.

On the contrary, by all accounts it will take another twenty years and $200 million to clean up. Meanwhile, UNICEF continues to drill tube wells on a global scale and has no documented and validated Standard Operating Procedures for their installation or ongoing testing to certify that the water produced meets WHO guidelines for safe drinking water.

UNICEF did not stay idle in the face of this disaster — it managed to make it worse. Not all wells were poisoned, so testing was begun to determine which ones were safe. The unsafe ones were marked with red paint and the safe ones with green. However, the field kit that was supplied for testing was inaccurate and many wells designated as safe were actually poisonous and a significant number that were declared unsafe were, in fact, perfectly safe.

The aid organisation's actions bred huge mistrust among the locals who had complained for a long time that they were seeing people with outbreaks of blisters on their hands — a symptom of arsenic poisoning — and were pretty much ignored.

A similar case of mismanagement was the introduction of oral rehydration therapy (ORT), which also arose from the Bangladesh cholera outbreak. ORT is a simple and effective treatment for dehydration associated with diarrhoea and consists of administering a mixture of salts and glucose.

By 1980, the effectiveness of ORT for acute diarrhoea was widely accepted, and between 1980 and 2006 it had decreased the number of worldwide deaths per year from five million to three million.

Although there is no doubt that the introduction of ORT saved millions of lives, soon after its introduction, independent researchers discovered that the concentration of sodium chloride and glucose being used was nearly twice that required for the safe and efficacious treatment of general diarrhoea.

For more than two decades, UNICEF and the WHO recommended the use of this too-high solution, which caused increased stool output and vomiting in patients and exacerbated the need for acute intravenous infusion therapy. When IV infusion therapy was delayed or unavailable, children died.

Despite numerous independent research studies which demonstrated that the original ORT formulation could result in adverse outcomes, including death, UNICEF and the WHO continued to recommend its use.

Finally, in 2002, the WHO and UNICEF recommended changing the formula to a lower sodium and glucose formulation, stating: 'New formula for oral rehydration salts will save millions of lives — Number of deaths and severity of illness will be reduced'.

In the developed world, if a drug or therapeutic treatment regime is shown to cause adverse healthcare outcomes, it is immediately recalled from the market. However, the WHO and UNICEF have not implemented a recall of the original solution. In fact, its Technical Bulletin No. 9 says: 'For more than twenty years UNICEF and WHO have recommended a single formulation of glucose-based ORT to prevent or treat dehydration due to diarrhoea — it has been proven effective and without apparent side effects.'

This is simply not true and seriously compromises the credibility and scientific integrity of the WHO and UNICEF.

UNICEF AND THE WHO ARE not the only organisations that have made these sorts of mistakes in the developing world. My intention is not to point the finger at individual organisations, but rather to highlight the fact that there need to be better quality controls in place before action is taken. Quality is necessary for the longevity of these aid projects. Quite simply, global healthcare interventions need better science and better ethics. Currently, aid organisations run from one alleged magic bullet to solve global healthcare problems to the next to satisfy their donors' hunger for action and success.

When the bed nets were trialled under clinically controlled conditions, they did show a small but uneconomical benefit, but those conditions didn't reflect what would happen in real life.

This is where the social anthropology becomes important. You have to acknowledge the reality of how people live their lives if you are going to give them a solution they can and will use. People in Malawi live in one room — they have to cook, eat and sleep there. The bed nets can't be left up, so they have to take them down and put them up again every day in this small space.

People have to get up and leave the safety of the net sometimes during the night. Mostly, though, it's just too damn hot to sleep under a bed net so they don't get used.

We now have enough evidence to say they don't work, but getting the organisations to buy into it is hard. It gets in the way of being able to say to donors: 'We have distributed this many bed nets thanks to your donation.' Ironically, simply spraying with DDT would have done the job, but DDT has such a bad reputation that it would never be a politically acceptable solution.

Bed nets have been used elsewhere, such as Zambia, which showed a 50 per cent reduction in malaria, and Eritrea where the drop was 80 per cent. But when you do a bit more research, you find both Zambia and Eritrea were spraying the inside of people's homes with a high concentration of DDT as well. I suggest that the result would have been the same in those countries even without the nets.

Equally tragic was the Life Straw Personal debacle. This was a personal water purification system — a straw with a mouthpiece and filters that purports to make water safe to drink even if it's got every pathogen known to man. Having spent most of my life as an analytical chemist and the other half designing state-of-the-art pharmaceutical-grade water purification systems, I knew that it didn't work. I arranged for *Consumer* magazine in New Zealand to do some testing. They made up a solution of 5 per cent raw sewage, sucked it up through the filters and found, as I predicted, that it does not produce water that is safe to drink.

Millions of these have been deployed by the major aid organisations because the manufacturer published data that says it works. It won't stop the major causes of diarrhoea — cryptosporidium, giardia and rotaviruses. It filters out some bacteria but not enough to provide safe drinking water as prescribed by the WHO.

It's causing more deaths because it lulls you into a false sense of security. You are more likely to drink from a contaminated water source than you would before because you think the Life Straw will protect you.

Even worse — someone is flogging knock-offs of this useless tool. They look just like the Life Straw but don't have anything in them at all. People pirate anything and everything in the developing world. Probably 25–50 per cent of drugs distributed are either subpotent or have nothing in them. There is no shortage, despite Fred Hollows' fervent wish, of people happy to make money out of sick people. It is a shambles out there.

THE ROLE OF THE MEDICINE Mondiale Ethical Science Group is to cut through the chaos with articles in the scientific journals pointing out what is wrong with these so-called remedies. It is intended to be a political group whose two main components are experts we can provide on an as-needed basis and a group consisting mainly of medical students who collect raw data. In the case of bed nets, they are collecting every single paper that has been written on their effectiveness.

The Ethical Science Group will also make better use of the media, because scientific papers have been written about some of these problems with no change happening. We need a public outcry that will make the likes of the WHO act. That's what happened over the ORT.

The group is headed by Dr Divya Dhar, who was named Young New Zealander of the Year when I was named New Zealander of the Year and is a protégée of mine. There are going to be lots of Divyas in the future.

'You can change the world,' I told her. 'You can do as much as I've done just by fixing the bed net thing. That's within your grasp. All you have to do is collect all the papers, get all your students at Dunedin, Auckland and the med school on to it.'

I'll show them how to do weighted analysis on them and when we've done that we'll get an academic to do some statistical analysis, all done in the proper scientific way so *The Lancet* can have it as a paper for publication. Then it will be on to the next cab off the rank: it might be the zinc tablets, it might be vitamin A.

We are working on a go/no-go gauge for measuring what happens with any intervention. Suppose we had a drug that cured malaria in five years? Big tick. But what are the effects of that? There will be all these extra people around who wouldn't have survived before, so there's going to be a burden in other areas, such as clean water and late-onset diseases. We're trying to think about the whole big picture as well as the little picture and make sure not only that the individual quality programmes are there but also that they don't have negative fallout somewhere else.

There's a failure effect model that's used in pharmaceutical manufacturing, where you look at the risks associated with an intervention. That's what was missing in the UNICEF water programmes. You note that people are collecting water from streams, which are a moving source with a risk of contamination, so you make everyone get their water from a single well. But if that fails due to bacteriological or chemical contaminants, then not just a few people get poisoned, everyone does. Aid organisations hold the fate of the world's sick and poor in their hands and, sadly, this trust is horribly misplaced.

IF YOU CURRENTLY, or intend to, donate to an aid organisation, the best advice I can give you is to ask serious questions about specific outcomes. How many lives are being directly saved by their actions? What are the real, tangible outcomes? If we challenge these organisations to be more transparent, we might further combat the promotion of poor-quality aid programmes.

Ask to see a copy of their in-country training manuals and SOPs. If they don't have any, that means they are making things up as they go along, and extemporaneous aid interventions always end badly. When I was twelve, my ambition was to get a nice sports car. When I was twenty-one I wanted to expand my business and make money. But once I finished the work with the lenses, I realised I could make global changes. It's an extraordinary thing to think that by the time I die, there could be thirty million people having the gift of sight thanks to something that I played around with on a sketchpad, and millions more alive because they got the right dose of medicine.

Every day I draw on experiences I have had to help this happen. When I speak to groups — which I do a lot — I identify with the guys at Wye College who inspired me to become engaged in life. They were career academic scientists who believed that they could make the world better through their research, because they were doing work in making resistant crops for use in developing countries. It's almost like God had this map with my journey on it, that he didn't tell me about. Why did he get me to work at an agricultural research centre to learn about insecticides? Why did he put me in a position where I had to design developed world products for developing countries and have the social viscera to know what they would be happy to use. I would be happy to use the lenses that we designed for modern cataract surgery and I would be happy to use the IV drip set or have Amelia put in my incubator when she was born. She would have been better off in my incubator than any other I know of.

I'm trying to take all of the stuff I've learnt and come up with an SOP not just for healthcare but for our society. The big question is: 'What should we be doing as a society to make us better?' We've lost the plot to some degree because we make 90 per cent of what we produce for our entertainment rather than our wellbeing.

It can be done. It happened with the lenses when we changed the perception of healthcare away from giving people those terrible glasses that the WHO had endorsed.

I have a great sense of urgency about both what I do with my family and what I do with the projects overseas. There will be millions of babies each year who die because they don't have access to good nutrition or good incubators. Just because of an accident of birth they shouldn't be abandoned, like the child of unfit parents who is put into an orphanage.

My parents named me Raymond Avery and the derivation of my name is 'protector of the little people'. I don't think my parents would have ever considered this, but it is a name I intend to live up to.

To all you dreamers out there, to all you crazy ones: trust me. One man can change the world, and I invite you to join me on a journey to make it better than we found it.

ACKNOWLEDGEMENTS

The Giants

*. . . if I have seen further than others it is because I have stood on
the shoulders of giants*

— SIR ISAAC NEWTON

Barry Cowan

Chris Williams

Chuck Feeney

Colin Murdoch

Fred Hollows

Sir Graeme Douglas

Hilary Holloway

Hugh Green

Ian Hickling

Isaias Fessahai

Jack Wise

John Terry

Neil Human

Oliver Dickie

Rabindra Shresthra

Sanduk Ruit

The Crazy Ones

. . . Here's to the crazy ones.
The misfits.
The rebels.
The troublemakers.
The round pegs in the square holes.

The ones who see things differently
They're not fond of rules.
  And they have no respect for the status quo.

You can praise them, disagree with them, quote them,
  disbelieve them, glorify or vilify them.
About the only thing you can't do is ignore them.
Because they change things.

They invent. They imagine. They heal.
They explore. They create. They inspire.
  They push the human race forward.

Maybe they have to be crazy.
How else can you stare at an empty canvas and see a work of art?
Or sit in silence and hear a song that's never been written?
Or gaze at a red planet and see a laboratory on wheels?

We make tools for these kinds of people.

While some may see them as the crazy ones,
 we see genius.

Because the people who are crazy enough to think
they can change the world are the ones that do.

— STEVE JOBS, US COMPUTER ENGINEER AND INDUSTRIALIST (1955 –)

Angela Griffen
Ben Smith
Bill Nairn
Brendan Lincoln
Bruce Jarvis
Charlotte Hurley
Claudia Caterwaul
Craig Getz
David Howse
David Ponting
David Waldon
Dean Woodall
Divya Dhar
Doug Lang
Eithne Curran
GisselleTrezevat-
  Miller

Graeme & Jan Tweedie
Graham Brewster
Ian Maxwell
James (Jim) Kennedy
  Grant
James Ferreira
Jan White
Jane Hunter
Jen Brown
Jim McKegg
Jo & Gareth Morgan
John Ashby
Jon Hooper
Josh Emett
Malcolm Bromley
Mark Olsen
Martyn Atack

Michael Nienaber
Milica Talic
Neil Finn
Oscar Kightley
Pak Peakocke
Paul Little
Peter & Prue Raos
Phil Augustin
Phil Smith
Richard Taylor
Rowan Simpson
Sam Morgan
Simon Blackwell
Sir StephenTindall
Stephen Murphy
Stuart McDonald
Tim Lightbourne

ABOUT THE AUTHOR

Ray Avery is a successful pharmaceutical scientist, a founding member of the Auckland University School of Medicine Department of Clinical Pharmacology, and former Technical Director of Douglas Pharmaceuticals who, over the past thirty years, has made a major contribution in the development of New Zealand's pharmaceutical industry.

However, it is Ray's ground-breaking work in the developing world that has brought him respect and recognition internationally.

As technical advisor to the Fred Hollows Foundation, Ray designed and commissioned two state-of-the-art intraocular lens laboratories in Nepal and Eritrea. Today, these laboratories supply 16 per cent of the world's market for intraocular lenses, and thanks to the innovative lens-manufacturing technology invented by Ray, the global cost of intraocular lenses has decreased to less than $6, making modern cataract surgery available to the poorest of the poor.

Working throughout Africa and Asia where he was exposed to the raw and real shortcomings in healthcare, Ray was determined to use his knowledge of pharmaceuticals, science, project management and product design to tackle big health issues endemic throughout the developing world at a very practical and sustainable level.

In 2003, Ray founded Medicine Mondiale and, using his contacts and charisma, he enlists the help of other scientists and social entrepreneurs to work with him.

Today an international network of scientists and technologists, together with New Zealand companies and Nobel laureates, support him and somehow everyone finds themselves donating their time and knowledge for free and they are rewarded by making a difference.

Ray has also invented the Acuset IV Flow Controller, which was a finalist in the 2008 Saatchi & Saatchi World Changing Ideas Award; Proteinforte, a revolutionary treatment for protein energy malnutrition; and a low-cost infant incubator specifically designed for use in the developing world.

His work has been recognised by his peers and he has received numerous awards including a Rotary Paul Harris Medal, the Bayer Research and Development Innovator Award 2008, World Class New Zealand Award for Biotechnology 2009, TBWA Disruption Award 2010, the Kiwibank New Zealander of the Year 2010 and the Blake Medal for Leadership 2010.

Ray is also the patron of the Non Resident Nepali Association of New Zealand, a position previously held by Sir Edmund Hillary, and he is the chair of the World Class New Zealand advisory committee.

FOR FURTHER INFORMATION ON THE WORK OF MEDICINE MONDIALE VISIT: *www.medicinemondiale.org*

DONATIONS TO MEDICINE MONDIALE

may be made online at
www.medicinemondiale.org
or by post to:

Medicine Mondiale
PO Box 67086
Mt Eden
Auckland
New Zealand